MarZar

AAT L3
Indirect Tax
Study Text and Exam Practice Kit

(For AAT assessments from January 2021)

Chapter	Contents	Page
1	Introduction to VAT	5
2	Types of Supply and VAT Registration	33
3	Normal and Special VAT Schemes	53
4	VAT Penalties and VAT Errors	69
5	VAT Invoices and Tax Points	83
6	Reclaiming VAT	103
7	Overseas Transactions	115
8	VAT Returns	125
	Solutions to Chapter Activities	147

Introduction

This Advanced level unit is about indirect tax: specifically, the tax that is referred to in the UK and throughout this unit as value added tax (VAT). The unit is designed to develop students' skills in preparing and submitting returns to the relevant tax authority in situations where the transactions that have to be included are relatively routine. However, some non-routine issues are also included in this unit.

This unit provides students with the knowledge and skills that they need to keep their employers and clients compliant with the laws and practices that apply to the indirect taxation of sales and purchases. The content is designed to ensure that students can perform these tasks relatively unsupervised, particularly in terms of routine and some nonroutine VAT tasks. However, it is expected that the student will still require some management for more involved and intensive VAT transactions. It is important that the student understands and applies the VAT rules from an ethical point of view. All VAT work must be carried out with integrity, objectivity and a high degree of professional competence. There must be due care with regard to confidentiality about any personal data being processed and, from a business protection aspect, with the correct approach to professional behaviour.

Students will learn about VAT legislation and the importance of maintaining their technical knowledge through monitoring updates. Students must be taught how to complete VAT returns accurately and must understand the implications of failing to do so. Inaccuracy and omission, late submission of returns and late payment or non-payment of VAT need to be understood in terms of the sanctions and penalties that are available to the relevant tax authority.

In particular, students will learn how to calculate the VAT value correctly in different circumstances, verify the calculations of the submitted return and correctly use an accounting system to extract relevant data for the return.

The VAT registration and deregistration rules are important aspects of learning at this level, and this includes the need to monitor sales closely to avoid breaching regulations. The existence and basic terms of special VAT schemes are also important.

Students will learn about how to deal with errors made in previous VAT returns and how and when these errors are corrected. They will also learn about communicating VAT matters to relevant individuals and organisations, including the special rules that apply when goods and services are imported into and exported out of the UK and the European Union (EU).

Indirect Tax is a mandatory unit.

Source: AAT Syllabus

Syllabus areas referenced to the study chapters (AQ2016 syllabus)

Learning outcomes	Chapters
Understand and apply VAT legislation requirements	1, 2, 3 & 5
Accurately complete VAT returns and submit them in a timely manner	4, 5, 6, 7 & 8
Understand the implications for the business of errors, omissions and late filing and payment	4 & 8
Report VAT-related information within the organisation in accordance with regulatory and organisational requirement	1, 4 & 8

This Study Text and Exam Practice Kit is produced by our expert team of AAT tutors. Our team have extensive experience teaching AAT and writing high quality study materials that enable you to focus and pass your exam. It covers all aspects of the syllabus in a user friendly way and builds on your understanding of each chapter by using real style exam activities for you to practice.

We also sell FIVE AAT 'real style' exam practice assessments for this subject to give lots more exam practice and the very best chance of exam success.

Visit www.acornlive.com/aat-home-study/ for more information.

Our team work very long hours to produce study material that is first class and absolutely focused on passing your exam. We hope very much that you enjoy our product and wish you the very best for exam success!

For feedback please contact our team aatlivelearning@gmail.com or safina@acornlive.com

Polite Notice! © Distributing our digital materials such as uploading and sharing them on social media or e-mailing them to your friends is copyright infringement.

1 Introduction to VAT

1.1 Introduction

This chapter will explain the following:

- That VAT is a tax on consumer spending and is charged on taxable supplies by a VAT registered business.
- That HMRC is the relevant tax authority for VAT.
- HMRCs rights in respect of inspection of records and visits to VAT registered businesses.
- HMRCs rules about what records should be kept, electronic invoicing and authorised accounting software.
- Electronic filing and digital tax return submission e.g. Maxing Tax Digital (MTD).
- The benefits of accounting software for identifying errors e.g. incorrect VAT rate, and the automation of calculations by using accounting software.
- Relevant sources of VAT information.

This chapter also covers aspects of professional ethics which are relevant to your syllabus:

- Identify when a query about VAT is beyond your current experience or expertise and so should be referred to a line manager.
- The importance of maintaining up-to-date and relevant VAT knowledge and the impact of this on the ability to act with professional competence.
- To deal with pressure to allow irrecoverable VAT or other inappropriate amounts to appear on the VAT return, or to remain in the accounts.

AAT reference material is available during your exam which will include most of the information that is covered in this chapter.

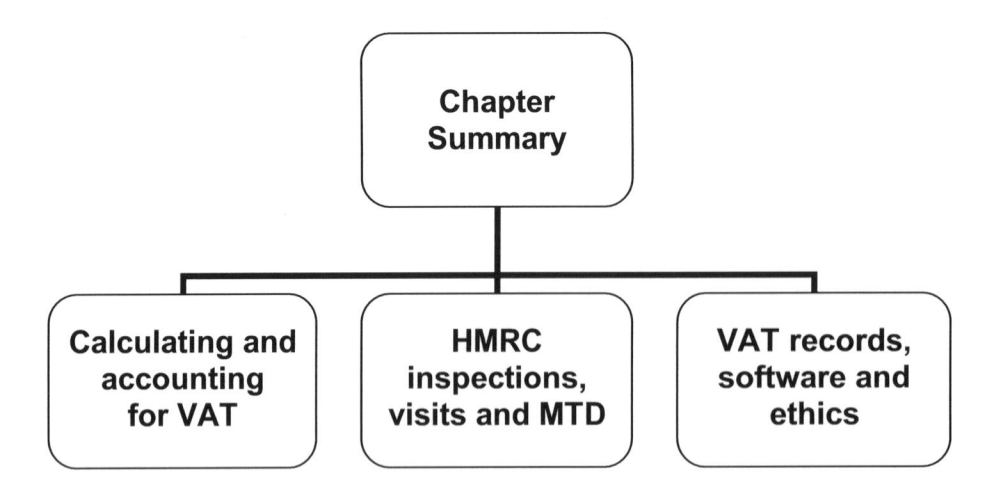

Chapter Summary

- Calculating and accounting for VAT
- HMRC inspections, visits and MTD
- VAT records, software and ethics

1.2 What is VAT

Her Majesty's Revenue and Customs (HMRC) is the government department and relevant tax authority responsible for operating the VAT system. VAT is a tax that is charged on most goods and services by a VAT-registered business in the UK. It can also be charged on goods and services that are imported from outside the UK.

VAT is a consumption (or expenditure) tax which is based on sales value and is known as an 'ad valorem' tax, which means 'according to value'. A VAT registered business charges VAT on the sale of most goods or services supplied in the UK, regardless of whether the sale is to another VAT registered business, or to another business or member of the public (end user), who are not VAT registered.

When a member of the public buys goods or services they may have to pay VAT, which is included in the sales price of what they spend. The VAT registered business would collect the VAT from the sales transaction and pay the amount to HMRC. The VAT is not suffered by the VAT registered business it is ultimately paid by the member of the public who is not VAT registered and cannot reclaim the VAT they have paid.

Output tax

VAT maybe charged when a VAT-registered business sells goods and services to a business or non-business customer in the UK.

- Outputs mean the total value of sales excluding VAT.
- Output tax is the VAT charged on the sale of goods and services supplied.
- Output tax is not a cost to a VAT registered business, it is a tax which is administered and collected by the business and paid to HMRC.
- Sales invoices and sales credit notes are used to account for output tax.

Input tax

VAT maybe paid when a business purchases goods and services from a VAT-registered business in the UK.

- Inputs mean the total value of purchases and all other expenses excluding VAT.
- Input tax is VAT which has been charged on the purchase price of goods and services supplied.
- A VAT registered business can normally reclaim any VAT it has paid on the purchase price of goods and services supplied.
- Purchases invoices and purchases credit notes are used to account for input tax.

Payments (or refunds) of VAT

A VAT-registered business normally completes a VAT return every 3 months.

- If output tax payable on sales is greater than input tax reclaimed on purchases, the business pays over the difference (VAT owing to HMRC).
- If input tax reclaimed on purchases is greater than output tax payable on sales, the business receives the difference (VAT owing from HMRC).

VAT is collected and administered by a VAT registered business, but the cost of any VAT is ultimately suffered by the general public (or a non-VAT registered business), who is unable to reclaim back any VAT they have paid on their purchase of goods or services.

Practice example

A wholesaler buys an item for £3,000 plus VAT and then sells it to a retailer for £7,000 plus VAT. The retailer sells the item for £15,000 plus VAT to a non-VAT registered person. The wholesaler and retailer are VAT registered. The rate of VAT is 20%.

How the VAT is collected and paid

Wholesaler   £

Buys item for £3,000 plus VAT:

£3,000 x 20% VAT =   -600   Input Tax

Sells it to retailer for £7,000 plus VAT:

£7,000 x 20% VAT =   1,400   Output Tax

Amount paid to HMRC   800

Retailer   £

Buys item from wholesaler for £7,000 plus VAT:

£7,000 x 20% VAT =   -1,400   Input Tax

Sells it to non-VAT registered individual for £15,000 plus VAT:

£15,000 x 20% VAT =   3,000   Output Tax

Amount paid to HMRC   1,600

Non-VAT registered individual

Buys item from retailer for £15,000 plus VAT of £3,000 = £18,000.

Cannot reclaim back the £3,000 VAT suffered.

VAT is charged on the sales price of the item as it passes from one party to another. The wholesaler and retailer were both VAT registered, so any VAT paid will not be a cost to either party, they can reclaim the VAT back from HMRC. The final cost of £3,000 VAT is ultimately paid by the individual, who is not VAT registered and unable to reclaim back the £3,000 VAT they have suffered.

1.3 Calculating VAT

Exam tasks may require you to identify VAT amounts where appropriate, from a figure that either includes or excludes VAT. The following examples illustrate VAT workings and calculations.

Working out VAT from a net amount (excluding VAT)

A sales amount is £2,500 (net) and VAT is to be calculated on the sale.

VAT is 20% of the net amount.

Using percentages, the amount is (£2,500 ÷ 100%) = £25 for every 1% x 20% = £500.

The VAT amount could also be calculated by multiplying the net sales amount by the fraction 20/100 and rounded to the lowest common denominator this is 1/5 as a fraction.

1/5 x £2,500 = £500.

The fraction 1/5 (1 ÷ 5) is 0.2 as a decimal.

0.2 x £2,500 = £500.

Working out VAT from a total gross amount (including VAT)

A sales amount is £3,000 (gross) and VAT is to be calculated on the sale.

As a percentage the amount of £3,000 represents 120% because 100% is the net sales amount and 20% has been added for VAT.

Using percentages, the amount is (£3,000 ÷ 120%) = £25 for every 1% x 20% = £500.

The VAT amount could also be calculated by multiplying the gross sales amount by the fraction 20/120 and rounded to the lowest common denominator this is 1/6 as a fraction.

1/6 x £3,000 = £500.

1.4 The day books (books of 'original' or 'prime entry')

Exam tasks may expect you to use the content of daybooks and distinguish between relevant and non-relevant data to construct a VAT return, or advise about the entries required in a VAT account.

The day books (books of 'original' or 'prime entry')

Day books keep a record of a business's past transactions and documents such as invoices, credit notes and bank receipts and payments. At the end of each period the day books are totalled, and the summarised totals posted to the general ledger accounts using the double entry system.

Day books (the books of 'original' or 'prime entry')

- Sales Day Book (SDB records sales invoices issued, for goods sold on credit to customers).

- Sales Returns Day Book (SRDB records credit notes sent to credit customers, to reverse sales invoice amounts issued to credit customers, due to goods returned from customers or disputes with customers).

- Discounts Allowed Day Book (DADB records credit notes sent to credit customers, to reverse sales invoice amounts issued to credit customers, due to prompt payment discounts allowed for customers to settle their invoices earlier).

- Purchase Day Book (PDB records purchase invoices, for goods purchased on credit from suppliers).

- Purchase Returns Day Book (PRDB records credit notes received from credit suppliers, to reverse purchase invoice amounts issued from credit suppliers, due to goods returned back to suppliers or disputes with suppliers).

- Discounts Received Day Book (DRDB records credit notes received from credit suppliers, to reverse purchase invoice amounts issued from credit suppliers, due to prompt payment discounts allowed by suppliers to settle purchase invoices earlier).

- Cash Book (CB records all cash and bank transactions of the business).

- Petty Cash Book (PCB records very small cash transactions of the business).

- Journal Book (JN records entries made to the general ledger, for period end adjustments and the correction of errors or omissions).

1.5 The VAT control account

The purpose of a VAT control account is to accurately record all VAT payable that has been collected from sales (outputs) and all VAT reclaimed from purchases and expenses (inputs). An accurate VAT balance can be calculated, and it provides all the necessary figures for a VAT return to be prepared by the business.

Exam tasks can require reasons why a VAT return balance does not agree with the balance in a VAT account and this will require good understanding of VAT control account entries.

A proforma VAT control account is shown below to illustrate the debit and credit entries. The balance brought down (b/d) is shown on the credit side because VAT is normally owed to HMRC and is a liability of the business, alternatively VAT can be an asset and the balance brought down (b/d) on the debit side, in which case VAT is owed from HMRC.

VAT control account

	£		£
Purchases daybook (PDB)	X	Balance b/d	X
Cash purchases (CB)	X	Sales daybook (SDB)	X
Cash expenses (CB)	X	Cash sales (CB)	X
Sales returns daybook (SRDB)	X	Purchases returns daybook (PRDB)	X
Discounts allowed daybook (DADB)	X	Discounts received daybook (DRDB)	X
Bank (payment of VAT to HMRC)	X	Bank (refund of VAT from HMRC)	X
Balance c/d	X		
	X		X
		Balance b/d	X

When making accounting entries to a VAT control account, think about the debit and credit entries in terms of what they do, they either increase VAT owed (credit entry to increase liability) or decrease VAT owed (debit entry to decrease liability).

Output VAT from cash sales or credit sales will increase liability to pay VAT (credit to increase liability). Credit notes for sales returns or discounts allowed to customers will reverse output VAT owed on sales and are the opposite entry (debit to decrease liability).

Input VAT reclaimed from cash expenses, cash purchases and credit purchases will decrease liability to pay VAT (debit to decrease liability). Credit notes for purchases returns or discounts received from suppliers, will reverse input VAT reclaimed on purchases and expenses and are the opposite entry (credit entry to increase liability).

A bank payment to HMRC for VAT due, would debit the VAT control account and credit the bank (credit to decrease asset). A bank receipt from HMRC for a VAT repayment, would debit the bank (debit to increase asset) and credit the VAT control account.

Practice example

The following details are from the day books of a business for the month of April. The VAT balance owed to HMRC on 1 April was £3,488. Prepare a VAT control account using the information shown below.

Cash book - credit side

Date 20XX	Details	Bank £	Trade payables £	Cash purchases £	VAT £	Other expenses £
12 Apr	DEF	1340	1340			
13 Apr	PQR	3600	3600			
22 Apr	Cash purchases	840		700	140	
28 Apr	Rent - SO	1500				1500
29 Apr	TUV	950	950			
30 Apr	Balance c/d	27870				
	Total	36100	5890	700	140	1500

Purchases day book (PDB)

Date 20XX	Details	Invoice number	Total £	VAT £	Net £
1 Apr	PQR	AB00987	2880	480	2400
2 Apr	DEF	0098256	672	112	560
13 Apr	DEF	0098519	480	80	400
24 Apr	TUV	1005	1068	178	890
26 Apr	PQR	AB01022	1440	240	1200
		Total	6540	1090	5450

Purchases returns day book (PRDB)

Date 20XX	Details	CN number	Total £	VAT £	Net £
4 Apr	DEF	00011	360	60	300
25 Apr	DEF	00023	792	132	660
		Total	1152	192	960

Discounts received day book (DRDB)

Date 20XX	Details	CN number	Total £	VAT £	Net £
13 Apr	PQR	AB001344	228	38	190
		Total	228	38	190

Cash book - debit side

Date 20XX	Details	Bank £	Trade receivables £	Cash sales £	VAT £
1 Apr	Balance b/d	15500			
12 Apr	ABC	9800	9800		
23 Apr	OMG	9600	9600		
24 Apr	Cash sales	1200		1000	200
	Total	36100	19400	1000	200

Sales day book (SDB)

Date 20XX	Details	Invoice number	Total £	VAT £	Net £
1 Apr	OMG	00987	6600	1100	5500
2 Apr	ABC	00988	4272	712	3560
13 Apr	OMG	00989	5400	900	4500
24 Apr	XYZ	00990	1656	276	1380
26 Apr	XYZ	00991	8040	1340	6700
		Total	25968	4328	21640

Sales returns day book (SRDB)

Date 20XX	Details	CN number	Total £	VAT £	Net £
4 Apr	ABC	0012	360	60	300
29 Apr	XYZ	0014	792	132	660
		Total	1152	192	960

Discounts allowed day book (DADB)

Date 20XX	Details	CN number	Total £	VAT £	Net £
23 Apr	OMG	0013	480	80	400
		Total	480	80	400

VAT control account

Date	Details	Amount £	Date	Details	Amount £
	Total			Total	

Picklist: Balance b/d, Balance c/d, Sales day book (SDB), Cash book (CB), Sales returns day book (SRDB), Discounts allowed day book (DADB), Purchases day book (PDB), Purchases returns day book (PRDB), Discounts received day book (DRDB).

The solution is on the next page.

Solution to practice example

The general ledger

VAT control account

Date	Details	Amount £	Date	Details	Amount £
30 Apr	CB (Cash purchases)	140	1 Apr	Balance b/d	3488
30 Apr	PDB	1090	30 Apr	CB (Cash sales)	200
30 Apr	DADB	80	30 Apr	SDB	4328
30 Apr	SRDB	192	30 Apr	PRDB	192
30 Apr	Balance c/d	6744	30 Apr	DRDB	38
	Total	8246		Total	8246
			1 May	Balance b/d	6744

The amount of VAT owed to HMRC (credit balance) on 30 April is £6,744.

Keeping a VAT account

AAT reference material available during your exam will include the information that should be kept in a VAT account (listed below) and there is no requirement to memorise this information.

A VAT account can be kept in whatever way suits the business best, so long as it includes information about VAT that it:

- Owes on sales, including when fuel scale charges are used.
- Owes on acquisitions from other European Union (EU) countries.
- Owes following a correction or error adjustment.
- Can reclaim on business purchases.
- Can reclaim on acquisitions from other EU countries.
- Can reclaim following a correction or error adjustment.
- Is reclaiming via VAT bad debt relief.

All the above information is covered in future chapters.

1.6 Inspection of records and visits by HMRC

A VAT officer can visit a VAT registered business to inspect their VAT records and make sure they are paying or reclaiming the right amount of VAT. HMRC will usually contact the business to arrange a visit and normally will give at least 7 days' notice.

HMRC will confirm before the visit what information they'll want to see (which records and the VAT periods they want to look at) and how long it's likely to take. A business can ask them to delay the visit. During the visit HMRC will work with the business to put right any problems with their VAT and also will inform the business about any additional tax and penalties they may have to pay. HMRC can also visit without an appointment and telephone the business about VAT matters.

What records should be kept

AAT reference material available during your exam will include all business records and VAT records that should be kept, there is no requirement to memorise this information.

A VAT-registered business must:

- Keep a record of its sales and purchases.
- Keep a separate summary of VAT (a VAT account).
- Issue correct VAT invoices.

Business records kept

- Annual accounts, including statements of profit or loss.
- Bank statements and paying-in slips.
- Cash books and other account books.
- Orders and delivery notes.
- Purchases and sales day books.
- Records of daily takings such as till rolls.
- Relevant business correspondence.

VAT records kept

- Records of all standard-rated, reduced-rated, zero-rated and exempt goods and services that are bought and sold.
- Copies of all sales invoices issued. However, businesses do not have to keep copies of any less detailed (simplified) VAT invoices for items under £250 including VAT.
- All purchase invoices for items purchased for business purposes unless the gross value of the supply is £25 or less and the purchase was from a coin-operated telephone or vending machine, or for car parking charges or tolls.
- All credit notes and debit notes received.
- Copies of all credit notes and debit notes issued.
- Records of any goods or services bought for which there is no VAT reclaim, such as business entertainment.
- Records of any goods exported.
- Any adjustments, such as corrections to the accounts or amended VAT invoices.

Electronic invoicing

Electronic invoicing is the transmission and storage of invoices in an electronic format without duplicate paper documents. The electronic format may be a structured format such as XML, or an unstructured format such as PDF.

How long VAT records should be retained

Generally, all business records that are relevant for VAT must be kept for at least six years. If this causes serious problems in terms of storage or other costs, then HMRC may allow some records to be kept for a shorter period.

How VAT records should be retained

A business can keep VAT records on paper, electronically or as part of a software program. Records may be stored digitally especially if needed to overcome storage and access difficulties. Records must be accurate, complete and readable. Digital records can be kept in a range of compatible digital formats, they do not all have to be held in the same place, or on one piece of software.

1.7 Maxing Tax Digital (MTD)

Making Tax Digital (MTD) is a key part of the UK governments plan to make it easier for an individual and business to get their tax right and keep on top of their tax affairs.

MTD requires that a VAT registered business uses electronic filing to submit VAT returns using MTD-compatible software and that it keeps digital business records. This now applies to the vast majority of businesses for VAT periods that started on or after 1 April 2019.

MTD does not require a business to keep additional records for VAT, but does require the business to keep records digitally. Digital records should include for each supply, the time of supply (tax point), the value of the supply (net excluding VAT) and the rate of VAT charged. Digital records should also include information about the business, including the business name, principle business address and VAT registration number.

MTD-compatible software

It is increasingly common for business records and accounts to be kept digitally on a computer, tablet, smart phone or cloud-based application. MTD-compatible software is required to keep digital records and communicate with HMRC digitally through the HMRC Application Programming Interface (API) platform. If a business currently does not use software, or its software is not MTD compatible, it will need to consider what software is suitable for its requirements.

Compatible software is any software product that supports the MTD obligations of keeping digital records and submitting data digitally using the MTD service. Digital records can be kept in a range of compatible digital formats. They don't have to be held in the same place or on one piece of software, a spreadsheet could be a key component for digital record keeping.

HMRC does publish details of VAT compatible software products, examples include:

- QuickBooks.
- Clear Books.
- FreeAgent.
- Sage Business.
- Xero.
- Zoho Books.

The submission of information to HMRC must always be via an Application Programming Interface (API). While HMRC expects most businesses to use API-enabled commercial software packages both to keep digital records and file their VAT Returns, bridging software or API-enabled spreadsheets may be used as an alternative.

Bridging software is a digital tool that can take information from other applications for example, a spreadsheet or an in-house record keeping system, and lets the user send the required information digitally to HMRC in the correct format. Bridging software acts as the 'bridge' between other applications and the HMRC portal for submitting VAT returns online.

Soft landing period

HMRC have allowed a "soft landing period" until 1 April 2021 for businesses to have in place digital links between all parts of their functional compatible software.

A 'digital link' is one where a transfer or exchange of data is made, or can be made, electronically between software programs, products or applications, without the involvement or need for manual intervention such as the copying over of information by hand or the manual transposition of data between two or more pieces of software.

During the soft-landing period only, where a digital link has not been established between software programs, HMRC will accept the use of 'cut and paste' or 'copy and paste' as being a digital link for these VAT periods.

A spreadsheet can be used to calculate or summarise VAT transactions and arrive at the VAT return information that needs to be send to HMRC. If the business uses spreadsheets to keep business records, it will need bridging software to make the spreadsheet MTD-compatible.

The process for signing up for MTD

Before signing up to MTD the business will need either:

- Compatible software that allows it to keep digital records and submit VAT Returns on-line, or
- Bridging software to connect non-compatible software (like spreadsheets).

To sign up to MTD the business needs the following information:

- The business email address.
- HMRC Government Gateway user ID and password.
- VAT registration number and latest VAT return.

The business should receive a confirmation email from HMRC within 72 hours of signing up.

Circumstances when a business does not need to follow MTD rules

HMRC expect that most businesses will be able to meet the legal obligations of MTD, but accept that it may not be possible for a small number of businesses to do so.

A business will not have to follow the rules for MTD if HMRC are satisfied that it is not reasonably practicable to use digital tools, such as computers, software and the internet to keep business records or submit VAT returns.

Practical reasons not to follow MTD rules include:

- It is not reasonably practicable for the business to use digital tools to keep business records or submit VAT Returns because of age, disability, remoteness of location or for any other reason.
- The business is subject to an insolvency procedure.
- The business is run entirely by practising members of a religious society or order whose beliefs are incompatible with using electronic communications or keeping electronic records.

HMRC will not give an exemption purely on the basis that reasonable effort, time and cost is involved to make the transition to MTD for example, buying new hardware and software and the cost of learning how to use it.

The benefits of accounting software

- Accounting software is more efficient and can save allot of time and money compared to manual (paper) bookkeeping systems. Data entry is simpler, faster and reduces duplication for example, when a sales invoice is raised all relevant parts of the software accounting system would be instantly updated in real-time. Manual book-keeping systems normally make the process of data entry much slower, they are more error prone and labour intensive.
- Errors can happen anywhere and everywhere which is the reason why accounting software is favoured over manual systems, software automation reduces opportunities for human error and can also help prevent errors. Accounting software can assist with identifying errors such as an incorrect VAT rate and can automate VAT calculations for greater accuracy.
- Digital systems help send and receive invoices much faster which reduce delays, documents can be stored digitally for easy access and allow the automatic transfer of data when using services such as on-line filing for VAT Returns.
- Accounting software can generate reports quicker and more accurately such as customer and supplier balances outstanding, sales, profit and VAT reports.

1.8 Relevant sources for VAT information

Most questions can be answered by referring to the VAT section of the HMRC website.

If the answer to a question is not on the HMRC website, the quickest and easiest way is to ring the VAT Enquiries Helpline where most VAT questions can be answered. A business can make a VAT enquiry online, by webchat or phone but should only call HMRC if a VAT enquiry is urgent.

The VAT General Enquiries helpline can answer most questions relating to VAT, but there may be times when it is more appropriate to write to HMRC.

This would apply if:

- The VAT information published by HMRC either on its website or other printed notices does not answer the question.
- The VAT General Enquiries helpline has advised the business to write in.
- There is still real doubt about how VAT affects a particular transaction.

Summary

1. Look up the answer first using the VAT section of the HMRC website.
2. Contact the VAT Enquires Helpline next, if no information can be found on the HMRC website, or you are still unsure.
3. Finally, write a letter to HMRC if advised to write in, or you still have real doubts over the answer.

1.9 Ethical principles for accountants

The code of ethics establishes the fundamental principles of ethics for professional accountants and can be remembered using the acronym 'PIPCO'.

- Professional competence and due care
- Integrity
- Professional behaviour
- Confidentiality
- Objectivity

Professional competence and due care

Members have a continuing duty to maintain professional knowledge and skill at a level required to ensure that a client or employer receives competent professional service based on current developments in practice, legislation and techniques. This principle requires attainment and maintenance of professional competence, such as continuing professional development (CPD) in order to remain up to date with changes in the technical environment. Your syllabus requires you to recognise the importance of maintaining up-to-date and relevant VAT knowledge and the impact of this on the ability to act with professional competence.

Members should act diligently and in accordance with applicable technical and professional standards when providing professional services. Diligence shows care and conscientiousness to rules, regulations and the task assigned, members should avoid at all cost being careless, casual and sloppy in their work. A member should carry out their work to the best of their ability, diligently and with due care.

A professional accountant should make their own limitations known to a client or employer when tasks or advice is required. A member should not undertake a task or provide advice if they do not possess an adequate level of competence or if without competence, then to be either supervised, instructed or have their work reviewed by someone who is competent.

Integrity

Members should be straightforward and honest (truthful) in all professional and business relationships. Transparency and fairness are important aspects of integrity. Transparency is about being open, honest and straightforward and when something goes wrong, to not try to hide it and be upfront about the issue. Fairness is about being impartial and treating others without favouritism or discrimination.

Professional behaviour

Members should comply with relevant laws and regulations and should avoid any action that discredits their profession. Professional behaviour is about complying with laws and regulations as a minimum requirement.

Confidentiality

Members should respect the confidentiality of information acquired as a result of their professional and business relationships and should not disclose any such information to third parties without proper and specific authority, unless there is a legal or professional right or duty to disclose.

Accountants are in a unique position of having legal or privileged rights of access to information about their clients or employers business for example, salary information, sales figures, major customers and unpublished financial statements. Confidential information acquired as a result of professional and business relationships should not be used for the personal advantage of members or other third parties.

The client or employer must be able to trust the accountant not to disclose anything about their business to anyone as it could be detrimental to their operations. It is recommended that legal advice should be sought before a member acts to avoid the risk of being sued. As a basic rule, members should not disclose any information without consent from their employer or client, they need to be discreet and consider whom disclosure can be made to.

Objectivity

Members should not allow bias, conflicts of interest or undue influence of others to override their professional or business judgement. A member must be sceptical and to 'doubt the truth', verify sources and the validity of information. Information must be factually sound and not subjectively presented for anyone else or for a members own personal advantage.

Breaching objectivity includes falsifying or producing misleading information and deliberately omitting information to mislead a user. Members should not be associated with any form of information which is materially false, misleading, recklessly provided, or incomplete. This includes information that becomes misleading by its own omission.

Examples of ethical conflicts

An 'overbearing' manager or client trying to compromise your integrity (honesty) by asking you to ignore some aspects of a VAT rule or account for VAT information falsely. This would be a breach of integrity and breach of professional behaviour if breaking the rules. This threat may also include dealing with pressure to allow irrecoverable VAT or other inappropriate amounts to appear on the VAT return or remain in the accounts.

Divided loyalties between close colleagues/clients/employers/relatives and adhering to professional standards. For example, overlooking a VAT accounting mistake a colleague has made because it could cost them their job.

Accepting a task without possessing the adequate expertise or experience to carry out the task assigned would be a breach of professional competence and due care. You must know when it is appropriate to obtain guidance from HMRC or seek expertise about VAT matters, particularly in respect of issues where there is doubt over the correct treatment.

You must be able to identify when a query about VAT is beyond your current experience or expertise and so should be referred to a line manager. A member should not undertake a task or provide advice if they do not possess an adequate level of competence or if without competence, then to be either supervised, instructed or have their work reviewed by someone who is competent.

Chapter activities

Activity 1.1

Show whether the following statements about VAT are true or false.

	TRUE	FALSE
Output VAT is charged by a VAT registered business, on its sales made to both other businesses and ordinary consumers.	☐	☐
Input tax can normally be reclaimed back by a VAT registered business from HMRC.	☐	☐
Business outputs are the total value of sales and all other outputs including VAT.	☐	☐

Activity 1.2

Calculate the VAT on the following sales figures that are excluding VAT. The VAT rate is 20%. Show your numerical answers to TWO decimal places.

(i) £27.75

£ ☐

(ii) £388.65

£ ☐

(iii) £49.95

£ ☐

Activity 1.3

Calculate the VAT on the following sales figures that are including VAT. The VAT rate is 20%. Show your numerical answers to TWO decimal places.

(i) £45.60

£ [   ]

(ii) £401.94

£ [   ]

(iii) £107.40

£ [   ]

Activity 1.4

A business has total purchases of £3,605.22 including VAT. The rate of VAT is 20%. Show all numerical answers to TWO decimal places.

The net purchases figure is.

£ [   ]

The VAT figure is.

£ [   ]

Activity 1.5

Show whether the following statements about VAT are true or false.

	TRUE	FALSE
Value added tax (VAT) is a tax charged on the sale of most goods or services in the UK by a VAT-registered business.	☐	☐
Inputs are the total value of purchases and all other inputs including VAT.	☐	☐
HMRC is the government department responsible for operating the VAT system.	☐	☐

Activity 1.6

Identify what type of software is a digital tool that acts as the middleman between other applications and the HMRC portal for submitting VAT returns online.

Bridging software	☐
MTD-compatible software	☐
Electronic invoicing	☐
Accounting software	☐

Activity 1.7

A wholesaler buys a good for £3,000 plus VAT of £600 and then sells the good to a retailer for £7,000 plus VAT of £1,400. The retailer sells the good for £15,000 plus VAT of £3,000 to a non-VAT registered business. Both the wholesaler and retailer are a VAT registered business. The rate of VAT is 20%.

Calculate the cost to each of the parties for the £3,000 VAT received by HMRC. If your answer is zero, enter '0'.

Cost to the wholesaler

£ [   ]

Cost to the retailer

£ [   ]

Cost to the non-VAT registered business

£ [   ]

Activity 1.8

A business recorded an invoice sent to a customer showing VAT of £1,270, the correct VAT amount that should have been recorded was £1,207. Currently the business's VAT account shows output tax of £6,230 and input tax of £1,380.

Identify which of the following figures will be shown in the business's VAT account when the error has been corrected.

Input tax £1,317	☐
Input tax £1,443	☐
Output tax £6,293	☐
Output tax £6,167	☐

Activity 1.9

The correct VAT payable by a business for the relevant VAT return period was £3,600. The VAT control account for the same period shows VAT payable of £3,045.

Identify which one of the following would explain this difference.

Output VAT of £555 was duplicated in the VAT control account	☐
Output VAT of £555 was omitted in the VAT control account	☐
Input VAT of £555 was omitted in the VAT control account	☐

Activity 1.10

Accepting a task without possessing the adequate expertise or experience to carry out the task assigned would be a breach of [⬇]

Picklist: Integrity, Confidentiality, Professional competence and due care.

End of Task

2 Types of Supply and VAT Registration

2.1 Introduction

This chapter will explain the different types of supply (sale) for VAT purposes:

Taxable supplies

- Standard-rated supplies.
- Reduced-rated supplies.
- Zero-rated supplies.

Non-taxable supplies

- Exempt supplies.
- Supplies outside the scope of VAT.

This chapter will also explain the VAT registration and deregistration requirements for a business:

- The VAT registration and deregistration requirements and thresholds.
- How to apply the historic turnover method and the future turnover method to comply with VAT registration and deregistration requirements.
- Circumstances when voluntary VAT registration may be beneficial for a business.

AAT reference material is available during your exam which will include most of the information that is covered in this chapter.

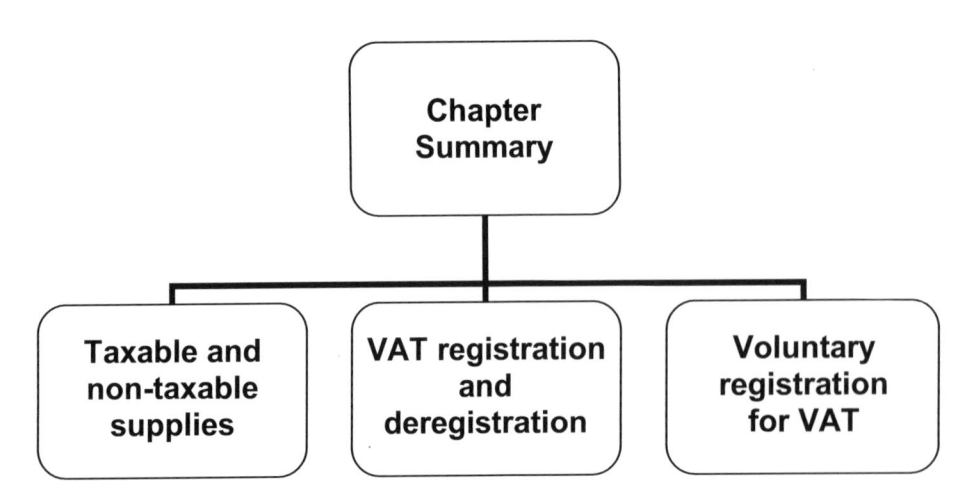

Chapter Summary
- Taxable and non-taxable supplies
- VAT registration and deregistration
- Voluntary registration for VAT

2.2 Types of supply

Taxable supplies (sales) include standard-rated (20%), zero-rated (0%) and reduced-rated (5%) goods and services. A taxable supply is any supply made in the UK which is not exempt from VAT. A VAT registered business must charge VAT on its taxable supplies.

Rates of VAT on taxable supplies depends on the type of goods or services supplied.

- Standard rated supplies - 20% VAT
- Reduced rate supplies - 5% VAT
- Zero rated supplies - 0% VAT

Your exam will always state whether sales (outputs) or purchases (inputs) are standard rated, zero rated or exempt. The 5% reduced rate for VAT calculations would not be examined. Most goods and services supplied in the UK are standard rated, some examples of zero rated and reduced rated supplies are shown below but there is no requirement to memorise any of them.

Reduced Rate Supplies (5% VAT rate)

A VAT registered business would charge 5% VAT on the sale.

- Children's car seats.
- Domestic fuel or power.
- Mobility aids for older people.
- Smoking cessation products e.g. nicotine patches and gum.
- Sanitary protection products.

Zero Rated Supplies (0% VAT rate)

A VAT registered business would charge 0% VAT on the sale.

- Some types of food bought in shops (not restaurants).
- Children's clothes and shoes.
- Transport e.g. bus and train fares.
- Newspapers and books.
- Water and sewerage services.
- Any export of goods to EU and non-EU countries.

A VAT registered business that makes zero rated supplies must charge 0% output VAT on the selling price for these type of goods or services sold. Input VAT can be reclaimed from purchases and expenses that relate to zero rated sales. A VAT registered business that makes wholly or mainly zero-rated sales, is likely to receive repayments of VAT from HMRC, because it reclaims input VAT on its purchases or expenses, but charges no output VAT to its customers on zero-rated sales.

A VAT registered business that makes wholly or mainly zero-rated sales does not need to register for VAT and can apply for 'VAT exemption'. The benefit is that the business can dispense with the need to account for VAT and keep VAT records. The drawback is that if the business receives regular repayments of VAT it will lose the cash-flow benefit.

Practice example

A business made the following types of supply.

- Standard rated sales £240,000 plus VAT.
- Zero rated sales £35,000.

Standard rated purchases and expenses were £180,000 including VAT. Included in the amount of input VAT was £14,000 that relates to zero rated sales made by the business.

Calculate the VAT payable to HMRC.

Solution to practice example

Output VAT charged on sales:

- Standard rated sales £240,000 ÷ 100% x 20% = £48,000 VAT.
- Zero rated sales £35,000 ÷ 100% x 0% = £0 VAT.

Input VAT reclaimed on purchases:

- Standard rated purchases and expenses were £180,000 including VAT.
- £180,000 ÷ 120% x 20% = £30,000 VAT.
- All input VAT can be reclaimed, if the purchases or expenses relate to taxable supplies. Standard rated and zero-rated sales are both taxable supplies, so all input VAT can be reclaimed.

VAT payable to HMRC:

- Output tax £48,000.
- Input tax £30,000.
- VAT payable to HMRC is £18,000 (£48,000 - £30,000).

Non-taxable supplies

Non-taxable supplies are goods and services that are either 'exempt' from VAT or 'outside the scope' of VAT. A VAT registered business must not charge VAT on non-taxable supplies.

Examples of exempt supplies and supplies outside the scope of VAT are shown below but there is no requirement to memorise any of these examples. Your exam will state whether sales (outputs) or purchases (inputs) are standard rated, zero rated or exempt. Goods and services that are outside the scope of VAT will not be examined.

Exempt Supplies

- Health care.
- Dental care.
- Education and training.
- Public postal services provided by the Royal Mail.
- Gambling.
- Burials and cremations.

Exempt supplies are not taxable supplies. Exempt means that VAT is not charged on the selling price for these type of goods or services. A business that makes wholly (100%) exempt supplies cannot register for VAT. Input VAT suffered on standard rated purchases and expenses that relate to exempt supplies (sales), cannot be reclaimed by the business because it is unable to register for VAT.

Supplies outside the scope of VAT

- Wages and salaries paid to employees.
- Welfare services provided by charities.
- Donations to a charity.
- Goods sold as part of a hobby.
- Charges levied by the government e.g. MOT testing, tolls and congestion charges.

Outside the scope of VAT means that VAT would not be charged on such transactions and these transactions are excluded when preparing a VAT return.

Summary of standard rated, zero rated and exempt supplies

Type of supply	Output VAT charged	Input VAT reclaimed
Taxable supplies		
Standard rated	20%	Yes
Zero rated	0%	Yes
Non-taxable supplies		
Exempt	VAT not charged	No

- If a business makes wholly (100%) exempt sales, it cannot register for VAT and therefore cannot reclaim any input VAT it suffers on standard-rated purchases or expenses.
- If a business makes zero-rated sales, it can reclaim any input VAT it suffers on standard-rated purchases or expenses. A VAT registered business that makes wholly or mainly zero-rated sales can apply to be exempt from VAT registration.

Partly exempt suppliers

A VAT registered business is partly exempt, if it sells both taxable supplies (standard-rated or zero-rated sales) and non-taxable supplies (exempt sales).

- The business would charge output VAT on its taxable supplies and reclaim input VAT paid on its standard-rated purchases and expenses, that relate to taxable supplies.
- The business would not charge output VAT on its exempt (non-taxable) supplies and normally cannot reclaim input VAT paid on its standard-rated purchases and expenses that relate to exempt supplies, unless this amount of input VAT is below the 'de minimis' amount.

De minimis means 'insignificant or trivial things'.

- If the amount of input tax that relates to exempt supplies is less than (or equal to) the 'de minimis' amount, then it can be reclaimed by the business.
- If the amount of input tax that relates to exempt supplies is more than the 'de minimis' amount, then it cannot be reclaimed by the business.

An exam task would explain whether input tax that relates to exempt supplies is above or below the de minimis amount, you are not required to know the de minimis amount, only the rule.

Practice example

A business made the following types of supply.

- Standard rated sales £240,000 plus VAT.
- Zero rated sales £35,000.
- Exempt sales £100,000.

Standard rated purchases and expenses were £180,000 including VAT. Included in the amount of input VAT is £4,000 that relates to zero rated sales and £3,000 that relates to exempt sales.

Calculate the VAT payable to HMRC if:

(a) The input tax in relation to exempt supplies is less than the de minimis amount.
(b) The input tax in relation to exempt supplies is more than the de minimis amount.

Solution to practice example

Output VAT charged on sales:

- Standard rated sales £240,000 ÷ 100% x 20% = £48,000 VAT.
- Zero rated sales £35,000 ÷ 100% x 0% = £0 VAT.
- Exempt sales £100,000 (non-taxable and no VAT charged).

Input VAT reclaimed on purchases:

- Standard rated purchases and expenses were £180,000 including VAT. £180,000 ÷ 120% x 20% = £30,000 input VAT. £3,000 input VAT relates to exempt sales, therefore £27,000 input VAT (£30,000 - £3,000) relates to taxable sales (standard and zero rated).
- £27,000 input VAT that relates to taxable sales (standard and zero rated) can be reclaimed.
- £3,000 input VAT that relates to exempt sales, can only be recovered if this amount is less than the de minimis limit.

VAT payable:

(a) If input tax of £3,000 is less than the de minimis limit, it can all be recovered:

- Output tax £48,000.
- Input tax £30,000.
- VAT payable to HMRC is £18,000 (£48,000 - £30,000).

(b) If input tax of £3,000 is more than the de minimis limit, none of it can be recovered:

- Output tax £48,000.
- Input tax £27,000 (£30,000 - £3,000 relating to exempt sales).
- VAT payable to HMRC £21,000 (£48,000 - £27,000).

2.3 VAT registration and deregistration

VAT registration is compulsory for a business, if either of the following conditions are satisfied:

- Taxable turnover will be more than £85,000 in the next 30-day period (future turnover method), or
- Taxable turnover was more than £85,000 over the last 12-month period (historic turnover method).

Taxable turnover means the total of all standard rated and zero-rated sales excluding any VAT, it does not include exempt (non-taxable) sales.

Both tests above can be performed at any time by the business and if either of the two tests are satisfied (not both) it is compulsory that the business must register for VAT. For example, taxable turnover may not be expected to be more than £85,000 in the next 30-days, but if it was more than £85,000 in the last 12-month period, then the business must register for VAT.

The future turnover method

A business must register if at any time it realises that its total VAT taxable turnover is going to be more than £85,000 in the next 30-day period. This test is applied at any time of the month and for any day of the year.

The historic turnover method

A business must register for VAT if its taxable turnover was more than £85,000 over the last 12-month period.

A business that expects its taxable supplies to drop back below the deregistration threshold (currently £83,000) in the next 12 months, can apply to stay unregistered. The business must write to HMRC with evidence that the incident is a one-off occurrence.

Practice example

A business has never had taxable turnover that was more than £85,000 in any previous 12-month period. On 27 January 20X1 the business was awarded a sales contract worth £120,000 in the next 20 days. The sales contract is a taxable supply for VAT purposes and the incident is not a one-off occurrence.

Should the business be registered for VAT?

Solution to practice example

The business never had taxable turnover that was more than £85,000 in any previous 12-month period, so using the historic turnover method, the business is not required to be registered for VAT. On 27 January 20X1, it realised that its taxable turnover will be more than £85,000 in the next 30-day period, so using the future turnover method, it is compulsory that the business registers for VAT. Registration must be within 30 days of 27 January 20X1.

Practice example

A business started trading on 1 January 20X4 and had the following taxable sales:

Month	£
31 Jan 20X4	20,000
28 Feb 20X4	60,000
31 Mar 20X4	70,000
30 Apr 20X4	75,000

Should the business be registered for VAT?

Solution to practice example

Month	£		£
31 Jan 20X4	20,000	Jan	20,000
28 Feb 20X4	60,000	Jan & Feb	80,000
31 Mar 20X4	70,000	Jan, Feb and Mar	150,000
30 Apr 20X4	75,000	Jan, Feb, Mar and Apr	225,000

Taxable turnover has never exceeded more than £85,000 in a future 30-day period, so using the future turnover method, the business is not required to be registered for VAT.

Taxable turnover did exceed £85,000 in the previous 12-months on 31 March 20X4. In just the last 3 months taxable turnover was £150,000 so using the historic turnover method, it is compulsory that the business registers for VAT. The business must register for VAT within 30 days of 31 March 20X4.

Practice example

A business started trading on 1 January 20X4 and had the following taxable sales:

Month	£	Month	£
31 Jan 20X4	3,000	31 Jan 20X5	21,000
28 Feb 20X4	2,500	28 Feb 20X5	17,000
31 Mar 20X4	2,800	31 Mar 20X5	18,500
30 Apr 20X4	4,300		
31 May 20X4	2,300		
30 Jun 20X4	5,900		
31 Jul 20X4	3,000		
31 Aug 20X4	6,200		
30 Sept 20X4	9,500		
31 Oct 20X4	8,300		
30 Nov 20X4	9,000		
31 Dec 20X4	7,900		
Total	64,700		

Should the business be registered for VAT?

The solution is on the next page.

Solution to practice example

Rolling sales in the previous 12 months	£
Jan 20X4 - Dec 20X4	64,700
Feb 20X4 - Jan 20X5	82,700
Mar 20X4 - Feb 20X5	97,200
Apr 20X4 - Mar 20X5	112,900

Workings for 12-month taxable turnover:

- Jan 20X4 to Dec 20X4 (£64,700 already totalled for this 12-month period).
- Feb 20X4 to Jan 20X5 £82,700 (£64,700 + Jan 20X5 £21,000 - Jan 20X4 £3,000).
- Mar 20X4 to Feb 20X5 £97,200 (£82,700 + Feb 20X5 £17,000 - Feb 20X4 £2,500).
- Apr 20X4 to Mar 20X5 £112,900 (£97,200 + Mar 20X5 £18,500 - Mar 20X4 £2,800).

Taxable turnover has never exceeded more than £85,000 in a future 30-day period, so using the future turnover method, the business is not required to be registered for VAT.

Taxable turnover did exceed £85,000 in the previous 12-months to 28 February 20X5. Taxable turnover was £97,200 for the 12-months to 28 February 20X5 so using the historic turnover method, it is compulsory that the business registers for VAT. The business must register for VAT within 30 days of 28 February 20X5.

VAT registration

When a business registers for VAT it will be sent a VAT registration certificate that confirms:

- The business VAT number.
- When to submit the first VAT return and payment.
- The effective date to start accounting for VAT.

From the effective date the business must:

- Keep VAT records and a VAT account.
- Charge the right amount of VAT.
- Pay any VAT due to HMRC.
- Submit VAT returns.

Consequences of failing to register on time for VAT

HMRC may charge a civil penalty if a business fails to notify them on time that it should be registered for VAT. The amount of penalty charged will depend on the amount of VAT due and how late the business registered. HMRC will look closely at the circumstances of each case and if a reasonable excuse exists for late registration the business will not be liable to a civil penalty.

HMRC will also expect the business to pay any output VAT that should have been charged on its taxable sales, during the time the business should have been registered for VAT. The business has two choices in respect of output VAT that was not charged on sales invoices during this period, it can either:

- Treat sales invoices as VAT inclusive and absorb any output VAT which should have been charged to its customers, or
- Account for VAT as an addition to the charges already invoiced to its customers and attempt to recover the VAT amount from its customers. Customers are not legally obligated to pay this VAT amount, so this is an unlikely option for the business.

The business will be able to reclaim input VAT during the time it should have been registered for VAT.

Practice example

Taxable turnover for a business exceeded the VAT registration threshold four months ago and the business has not registered for VAT. Since this time the business invoiced £60,000 for goods sold to customers, all goods were standard rated supplies.

Solution to practice example

Two choices exist for how output VAT should be accounted for:

Treat the sales invoices as VAT inclusive and the business absorbs the VAT.

- £60,000 ÷ 120% x 20% = £10,000 Output VAT.

This option chooses not to recover VAT amounts from its customers. This is the worse option because the business will have to pay £10,000 VAT over to HMRC itself and so will damage the cash-flow of the business.

Account for VAT as an addition to charges already invoiced to customers.

- £60,000 ÷ 100% x 20% = £12,000 Output VAT.

This is a better option because the £12,000 VAT can be collected from invoicing customers for the VAT amount that was not previously charged and will cost the business nothing. However, customers are under no legal obligation to pay this VAT amount which means this option is often very limited for the business.

Voluntary registration for VAT

A business can voluntarily register for VAT even when its taxable turnover is equal to or less than £85,000. A business cannot register for VAT if it makes wholly (100%) exempt supplies.

Benefits of voluntary registration

- Reclaim input VAT on purchases and expenses which will benefit cash-flow.
- Improve credibility and image of the business. Even when sales are low, issuing VAT invoices to customers can make the business appear larger.
- No risk of sales accidentally going over the VAT threshold and getting into trouble.

Drawbacks of voluntary registration

- VAT registration can be an administration burden and may impose costs on the business. Any business voluntarily registering for VAT is required to comply with the rules for Making Tax Digital (MTD), which includes electronic filing of VAT returns (using MTD-compatible software) and keeping digital business records.
- The business must charge VAT on its taxable sales and this can be a problem if its customers are not VAT registered, because they would be unable to reclaim the VAT charged. The business could either add the full amount of VAT to the selling price, but this can damage competitiveness, or keep its selling prices the same and absorb the cost of the VAT itself, but this can worsen cash-flow.

Deregistration for VAT

A business can request that HMRC cancel its VAT registration if its VAT taxable turnover falls below the deregistration threshold of £83,000, however the business may still want to remain voluntarily registered for VAT. VAT registration must always be cancelled if the business is closed down or ceases to make taxable supplies.

A business can request that HMRC cancel its registration if:

- Taxable turnover in the previous 12 months is less than or equal to £83,000, or
- Taxable turnover in the next 12 months is expected to fall to £83,000 or less.

Taxable turnover means the total of all standard rated and zero-rated sales excluding any VAT, it does not include exempt (non-taxable) sales. Both tests can be performed at any time by the business and if either test is satisfied (not both), the business can deregister for VAT.

- It will normally take 3 weeks for HMRC to confirm cancellation.
- HMRC will send confirmation of deregistration for VAT.
- The business must stop charging VAT and will submit a final VAT return for the period up to its cancellation date.

Making Tax Digital (MTD)

VAT-registered businesses with a taxable turnover above the VAT threshold are required to use the MTD service to keep records digitally and use software to submit their VAT Returns.

If a business is required to register for MTD as a result of having taxable turnover above the registration threshold, it must continue to keep digital records and submit its returns digitally even if it falls below the VAT registration threshold at a future point in time. This obligation does not apply if the business deregisters from VAT or meets other exemption criteria.

If a business is exempt from MTD because taxable turnover is below the VAT registration threshold it may still choose to follow the Making Tax Digital rules. The business must notify HMRC in writing before the start of the VAT period in which it wishes to start using MTD. If a business has started using MTD voluntarily, and later decides it no longer wishes to follow the MTD rules, it must notify HMRC in writing and will no longer be required to follow the MTD rules from the start of the next VAT period after notification to HMRC.

Chapter activities

Activity 2.1

A business failed to register for VAT when it was required to do so. During this period, it made standard rated sales of £36,000.

If the business chooses to treat the invoices as VAT inclusive and absorb the VAT, the VAT amount would be:

£ [   ]

If the business chooses to recover the VAT from its customers, the VAT amount would be:

£ [   ]

Complete the following sentence.

The business may face a [   ] because it did not register for VAT when it is was required to do so.

Picklist: Prison sentence, Civil penalty, Criminal prosecution.

Activity 2.2

Show whether the following statements are true or false.

	TRUE	FALSE
It is mandatory for a business that makes wholly exempt supplies to follow MTD rules.	☐	☐
It is mandatory for a VAT-registered business with a taxable turnover above the VAT registration threshold to follow MTD rules.	☐	☐
It is mandatory for a VAT-registered business with a taxable turnover below the VAT registration threshold to follow MTD rules.	☐	☐

Activity 2.3

Business A sells goods to business B who in turn resells goods to business C.

Business A

- Zero rated sales £350,000 to Business B.
- Standard rated purchases £240,000 excluding VAT.

Business B

- Standard rated sales £750,000 inclusive of VAT to Business C.
- Standard rated purchases £60,000 excluding VAT.
- Zero rated purchases £350,000.

Business C

- Standard rated sales £1,500,000 excluding VAT to the general public.
- Standard rated purchases £625,000 excluding VAT.

Calculate the VAT payable to HMRC or reclaimable from HMRC for each business. Enter a negative figure if VAT is reclaimable from HMRC.

Business A

£ [-48,000]

Business B

£ [113,000]

Business C

£ [175,000]

Activity 2.4

A business makes only zero-rated sales.

Show whether the following statements are true or false.

	TRUE	FALSE
Zero-rated goods and services count as taxable supplies and are part of taxable turnover.	☐	☐
The business cannot register for VAT.	☐	☐
The business can apply to HMRC to be exempt from registering for VAT.	☐	☐

Activity 2.5

A business is partly exempt for VAT purposes and has input VAT which it wants to reclaim for its VAT return. Input VAT in connection with taxable and exempt sales include the following:

	Input VAT
Standard Rated Supplies	£35,000
Zero Rated Supplies	£10,000
Exempt Supplies	£2,000

Input tax in relation to exempt supplies made is less than the de minimis limit.

Complete the following statement.

The amount of input VAT that can be reclaimed by the business is [⬇]

Picklist: All of it, Some of it, None of it.

Activity 2.6

A business started to trade on 1 January 20X5.

The business makes a mixture of sales of both standard-rated and exempt supplies. The business sales are spaced evenly throughout the year at £30,000 per month. 40% of all sales each month are exempt supplies.

By which month must the business apply to be registered for VAT.

31 March 20X5	☐
31 April 20X5	☐
31 May 20X5	☐

Activity 2.7

Which of the following is a non-taxable supply.

Zero-rated sales	☐
Reduced rate sales	☐
Exempt sales	☐
Standard rated sales	☐

End of Task

3 Normal and Special VAT Schemes

3.1 Introduction

This chapter will explain the following:

- The timing and frequency of filing quarterly VAT returns and payments (or repayments) under the normal VAT scheme.
- The circumstances that monthly VAT returns may be beneficial to the business.
- The thresholds and qualification criteria for special VAT schemes, such as the annual accounting scheme, cash accounting scheme and flat rate scheme. The timing and frequency of filing VAT returns and payments (or repayments) under special VAT schemes. The circumstances for voluntary and compulsory withdrawal from special VAT schemes.

AAT reference material is available during your exam which will include most of the information that is covered in this chapter.

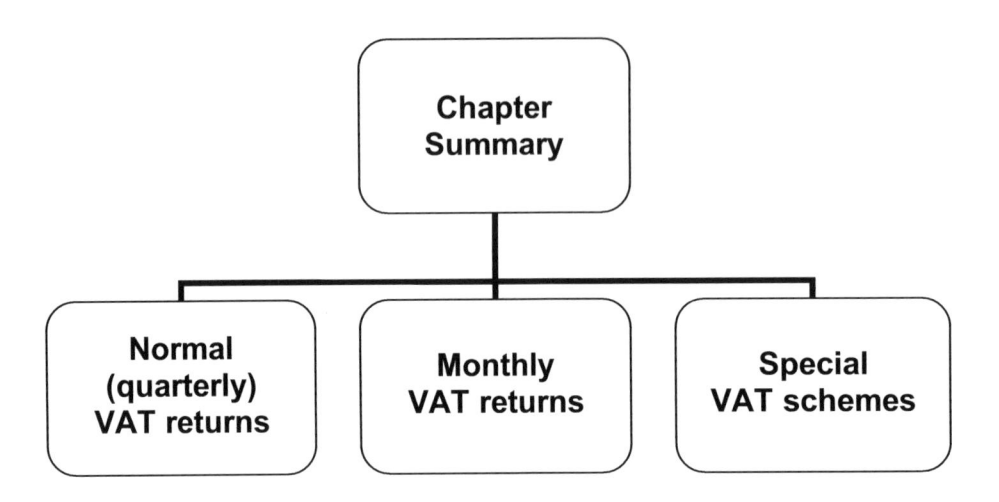

Chapter Summary

- Normal (quarterly) VAT returns
- Monthly VAT returns
- Special VAT schemes

3.2 VAT returns under the normal scheme

VAT transactions that are relevant to each VAT period end must be submitted and the VAT payment made to HMRC by the due date. VAT return period ends normally account for VAT transactions every quarter (every 3 calendar months).

The relevant period end dates to account for VAT are determined when the business first registers for VAT, however a business may choose to change these dates for example, to match a VAT period end date with the accounting year end of the business, or because a certain VAT period end is inconvenient for the business.

Monthly VAT Returns

VAT Returns are normally prepared quarterly, however monthly VAT returns can be allowed by HMRC for 'regular repayment traders'. These are businesses that receive regular repayments of VAT from HMRC for example, if a business makes wholly or mainly zero-rated sales, it has little or no output VAT to collect on its sales, but it still reclaims input VAT on its standard-rated purchases, so it most likely receives regular repayments of VAT from HMRC.

Monthly VAT returns help improve business cash flows because they enable a business to get back its VAT faster. The due date for submitting monthly VAT returns and making payments for VAT due is determined in the same way as preparing quarterly returns.

Submitting VAT Returns and paying VAT due

It is mandatory for virtually all VAT registered traders to submit their VAT Returns to HMRC using online filing and to pay any VAT due to HMRC electronically. A VAT registered business with a taxable turnover above the VAT threshold, is required to use Making Tax Digital (MTD) services, which means they have to keep records digitally and use software to submit their VAT Returns.

Key dates for VAT Returns

- The deadline for submitting the VAT return and paying the VAT due is the same.
- The normal due date for paper VAT returns is one calendar month after the end of the relevant VAT period.
- Online filing and electronic payment give the business an extension of an extra seven calendar days, in addition to the normal due date.
- If the business has a Direct Debit scheme in place with HMRC, payment will be automatically collected from the business bank account, three bank working days after the due date. Bank working days do not include weekends or bank holidays.
- Failing to pay VAT due on time may incur a civil penalty for late payment.

Practice example

A business uses online filing and electronic payment of VAT. It is currently preparing its VAT Return for the quarter ended 31 March 20X7. The business does not have a direct debit scheme in place with HMRC.

Solution to practice example

The VAT return must be submitted by 7 May 20X7 (31 March 20X7 + one calendar month + extra seven days). The due date for VAT payment is the same date 7 May 20X7. This solution would be identical if the VAT return was for the month ended 31 March 20X7.

Practice example

A business uses online filing and electronic payment of VAT. It is currently preparing its VAT Return for the quarter ended 31 March 20X7. The business has a direct debit scheme in place with HMRC.

Solution to practice example

The VAT return must be submitted by 7 May 20X7 (31 March 20X7 + one calendar month + extra seven days). The due date for VAT payment is the same date 7 May 20X7.

If the business pays by Direct Debit, HMRC automatically collects payment from the business bank account, three bank working days after the due date 7 May 20X7. Assuming no weekends or bank holidays in the 3 days after 7 May 20X7, the money will be collected by HMRC on 10 May 20X7 at the earliest.

This solution would be identical if the VAT return was for the month ended 31 March 20X7.

3.3 The Annual Accounting Scheme for VAT

A VAT registered business normally submits its VAT Returns quarterly (four times a year). Using the Annual Accounting Scheme for VAT a business can submit one VAT Return every year to HMRC. The business is still expected to comply with Making Tax Digital (MTD) rules.

The Annual Accounting Scheme

- One VAT Return submitted every year to HMRC and annual accounting for VAT.
- To avoid a huge annual VAT bill at the end of each year, the business makes nine fixed monthly payments in advance, towards its annual VAT bill at the end of the year. The fixed monthly payments are based on the previous year's VAT bill.
- When the annual VAT Return is submitted the business pays any final balance of VAT payable, or receives a VAT repayment for the year.

A business can start on the annual accounting scheme if its estimated taxable turnover during the next tax year is not more than £1.35 million. A business already using the annual accounting scheme can continue to do so until its estimated taxable turnover for the next tax year exceeds £1.6 million. A business must leave the scheme if its taxable turnover is (or is likely to be) more than £1.6 million for the next tax year.

At the same time as using the annual accounting scheme, the business may also use either the cash accounting scheme or the flat rate scheme (see later).

Benefits of Annual Accounting Scheme

- One VAT Return to submit each year.
- The due date to submit the VAT Return and pay the final balance of VAT due is two calendar months after the year end (longer deadline than monthly or quarterly returns).
- Certainty of cash flow because most of the VAT is paid in nine fixed monthly instalments during each year.

Drawbacks of Annual Accounting Scheme

- The scheme does not suit a business that regularly receives repayments of VAT because the business will only receive one refund of VAT each year (when it submits its annual VAT Return). A business that makes wholly or mainly zero-rated sales (a repayment trader) may therefore not find this scheme unsuitable.
- If taxable turnover decreases during the year, the fixed monthly instalments paid in advance could be higher than the annual VAT bill for the year. This is bad for cash-flow because the business will overpay VAT during the year and must wait until the end of the year to receive the balance of any VAT refund.

Practice example

A business uses the Annual Accounting Scheme for VAT. The VAT Return for the year ended 31 March 20X1 has been prepared and the VAT liability for the year is £31,299. The business paid nine fixed monthly instalments of £2,500 towards its VAT liability during the year.

Solution to practice example

- The annual VAT Return is due by 31 May 20X1 (31 March 20X1 + two calendar months).
- The final payment of VAT (also due by 31 May 20X1) is £8,799 (£31,299 annual VAT liability - 9 x £2,500 monthly payments made in advance).

3.4 The Cash Accounting Scheme for VAT

The VAT cash accounting scheme is one of the most popular VAT schemes available and offers some of the best cash flow benefits to a small business. When using normal VAT accounting, the supply date or invoice date for each VAT transaction normally determines the relevant VAT period to account for each transaction. This means that output VAT is normally paid on sales invoices issued in a relevant VAT period, whether or not the customer has actually paid, and input VAT is normally reclaimed on purchases invoices issued, whether or not the business has actually paid the supplier.

The cash accounting scheme

- Output VAT is not payable until the customer has paid the sales invoice. So, if a customer never pays the sales invoice, the business never pays the output VAT.
- Input VAT is not reclaimed until the business has paid the purchase invoice. So, if the business never pays the purchase invoice, the business never reclaims the input VAT.

Cash accounting can be used if the estimated taxable turnover of the business during the next tax year is not more than £1.35 million. A business can continue to use cash accounting until its taxable turnover exceeds £1.6 million. A business must leave the scheme if its taxable turnover is (or is likely to be) more than £1.6 million during the next tax year.

A business can join both the cash accounting scheme and annual accounting scheme. If a business joins both schemes, it accounts for VAT only on its cash receipts and payments and completes one annual VAT Return each year.

Benefits of Cash Accounting Scheme

- Using cash accounting can improve cash flow, especially if customers are slow payers because the payment of output VAT is not made until the customer pays.
- If a business has a bad debt it will never need to pay the output VAT because the customer has never paid.

Drawbacks of Cash Accounting Scheme

- If the business purchases most goods and services on credit terms, it cannot reclaim VAT on its purchases until it has paid the invoices.
- A business that makes wholly or mainly zero-rated sales is usually a repayment trader, but cannot reclaim input VAT until its purchases invoices have been paid.
- Joining the cash accounting when a business first starts to trade, would mean it is unable to reclaim VAT on any business start-up expenditure, such as inventory, tools or machinery, that it previously has paid for.
- If a business leaves the cash accounting scheme it will have to account for all outstanding output VAT payable, including output VAT on bad debts.

Practice example

A business is preparing its VAT return for the quarter ended 31 May 20X5.

Purchases day book

Invoice Date	Details	Invoice number	Total £	VAT £	Net £	Date paid
1 Apr 20X5	PQR	AB00987	2,880	480	2,400	22 May 20X5
22 Apr 20X5	DEF	0098256	672	112	560	24 May 20X5
13 May 20X5	DEF	0098519	480	80	400	24 Jun 20X5
		Total	4,032	672	3,360	

Sales day book

Invoice Date	Details	Invoice number	Total £	VAT £	Net £	Date received
13 Mar 20X5	OMG	0000913	6,000	1,000	5,000	22 May 20X5
23 Apr 20X5	LOL	0000914	6,720	1,120	5,600	24 Jun 20X5
21 May 20X5	LOL	0000915	4,800	800	4,000	24 Jun 20X5
		Total	17,520	2,920	14,600	

Using normal accounting rules for VAT

- VAT is accounted for on sales invoices issued in the relevant VAT period (1 March 20X5 to 31 May 20X5), whether or not the customer has paid. All output VAT of £2,920 is accounted for on sales invoices issued that relate to the relevant VAT period.
- VAT is accounted for on purchase invoices issued in the relevant VAT period (1 March 20X5 to 31 May 20X5), whether or not the supplier has been paid. All input VAT of £672 is accounted on purchase invoices issued that relate to the relevant VAT period.
- Using normal VAT accounting rules, VAT payable to HMRC for the quarter ended 31 May 20X5 is £2,248 (Output VAT of £2,920 less Input VAT of £672).

Using cash accounting rules for VAT

Purchases day book

Invoice Date	Details	Invoice number	Total £	VAT £	Net £	Date paid
1 Apr 20X5	PQR	AB00987	2,880	480	2,400	22 May 20X5
22 Apr 20X5	DEF	0098256	672	112	560	24 May 20X5
		Total	3,552	592	2,960	

Sales day book

Invoice Date	Details	Invoice number	Total £	VAT £	Net £	Date received
13 Mar 20X5	OMG	0000913	6,000	1,000	5,000	22 May 20X5
		Total	6,000	1,000	5,000	

VAT is accounted for in the relevant VAT Return period (1 March 20X5 to 31 May 20X5) only when cash is received or when cash is paid.

- Output VAT of £1,000 would be accounted for on sales invoice 0000913 because this sales invoice was paid by the customer on 22 May 20X5. All other sales invoices were not paid by customers in the relevant VAT period.
- Input VAT of £592 would be accounted on purchase invoices AB00987 and 0098256, because these purchase invoices were paid for by the business on 22 May 20X5 and 24 May 20X5. All other purchase invoices were not paid to suppliers in the relevant VAT period.
- Using VAT cash accounting rules, the VAT payable to HMRC for the quarter ended 31 May 20X5 is £408 (Output VAT of £1,000 less Input VAT of £592).

3.5 The Flat Rate Scheme for VAT

The amount of VAT a business pays to or reclaims back from HMRC is normally determined as the difference between the output VAT payable on taxable sales and the input VAT reclaimed on taxable purchases. This situation is the same regardless of whether cash accounting or normal accounting rules are used for VAT.

A business can simplify its VAT accounting by registering for the Flat Rate Scheme. This scheme allows a business to simplify the calculation of its VAT payments. VAT payments are calculated using a flat (fixed) rate percentage of the total VAT-inclusive turnover of the business. The total VAT-inclusive turnover of the business includes exempt, zero rated and standard rated sales (including VAT). There is no reclaim of any input VAT allowed if using the flat rate scheme.

The flat rate scheme

- To join the scheme the annual VAT-exclusive taxable turnover of the business must be £150,000 or less. Once the business has joined the scheme, the business can continue to use it until its total VAT-inclusive turnover exceeds £230,000.
- The flat rate percentage to calculate VAT payments depends on the type of business, however the maximum would be 16.5% charged by HMRC on total VAT-inclusive turnover (sales). The exam task would always state the flat rate percentage whenever relevant to completing an exam task.
- The business still issues sales invoices in the normal way to its customers and charges VAT on invoices in the normal way for any taxable supplies it makes.
- The business cannot reclaim input VAT on purchase invoices from suppliers, except for certain capital assets over £2,000 (see later).

The flat rate scheme can simplify and reduce the time needed to work out and account for VAT for a business. The business does not need to record entries in a VAT account such as output VAT it has charged on sales or input VAT it has paid on purchases.

A business can join both the flat rate scheme and annual accounting scheme. If a business joins both schemes, it would apply a flat rate percentage to its total VAT-inclusive turnover to calculate its VAT payment annually and submit one VAT return each year.

Practice example

A business uses the flat rate scheme for VAT. It is preparing its VAT return for the quarter ended. The VAT transactions for the relevant return period are shown below. The flat rate percentage for this type of business is 8%.

Purchases

Type of supply	Total £	VAT £	Net £
Standard rated	2,880	480	2,400
Zero rated	560	0	560
Exempt	400	0	400
	3,840	480	3,360

Sales

Type of supply	Total £	VAT £	Net £
Standard rated	9,600	1,600	8,000
Zero rated	6,000	0	6,000
	15,600	1,600	14,000

Normal accounting rules for VAT

- Output VAT of £1,600 is payable on standard rated sales that relate to the relevant VAT period.
- Input VAT of £480 is reclaimed on standard rated purchases that relate to the relevant VAT period.
- VAT payable to HMRC for the quarter ended is £1,120 (Output VAT of £1,600 less Input VAT of £480).

Flat rate scheme for VAT accounting

- The exam task will always state the flat rate percentage whenever relevant to completing an exam task. The VAT flat rate percentage for this type of business is 8%.
- Total VAT payable to HMRC is VAT-inclusive turnover (£15,600) x 8% = £1,248.
- The business cannot reclaim input VAT (£480) on purchase invoices from suppliers.

In the situation above, the business would be worse off if it joins the flat rate scheme. It would pay £1,248 VAT due using the flat rate scheme compared with £1,120 VAT due if using normal VAT accounting rules. The flat rate scheme is not designed to save money for a business it is designed to simplify its VAT accounting. It is advised that a professional accountant or tax advisor assess whether the business is better off or worse off before it registers for the scheme.

Limited cost business

If a business spends a very small amount on the purchase of goods, it may be classed as a 'limited cost business'. A limited cost business purchases goods that cost less than either:

- 2% of its turnover, or
- £1,000 a year.

A limited cost business, if it joins the flat rate scheme, will pay the highest flat rate percentage of its total VAT-inclusive turnover to calculate its VAT due to HMRC, which is currently a maximum of 16.5%. The reason is that if its purchases are relatively small, then the business under normal accounting rules would not reclaim much input VAT so could otherwise save allot of VAT if it joined the flat rate scheme.

Reclaiming VAT on capital expenditure

Normally under the flat rate scheme no input VAT is allowed to be reclaimed on purchases, any relevant amount is already considered in the calculation of the flat rate percentage issued by HMRC. However, the business may be able to reclaim input VAT that has been charged on capital expenditure, if it meets certain qualifying conditions. To reclaim input VAT on any capital expenditure, it must be a single item purchased, that costs £2,000 or more (including VAT) and is a good (not a service). All three conditions must be satisfied, otherwise any input VAT on capital expenditure cannot be reclaimed.

Benefits of Flat Rate Scheme

- Using the flat rate scheme can save time and simplify VAT accounting.
- The business gets a 1% discount on its flat rate percentage in its first-year anniversary as a VAT-registered business.
- Fewer VAT accounting rules to follow and peace of mind that there is less chance of mistakes when calculating VAT payable.

Drawbacks of Flat Rate Scheme

VAT payable could be higher than normal VAT accounting rules for the following reasons:

- If the business purchases wholly or mainly standard-rated items, it may not get the full cash-flow benefit if joining the flat rate scheme, it is unable to reclaim any input VAT.
- If the business regularly receives VAT repayments, for example sells wholly or mainly zero-rated goods or services, it will not receive repayments if joining the flat rate scheme.
- If the business sells mainly exempt or zero-rated supplies, under normal VAT accounting rules it would not pay output VAT due on these types of supply. When using the flat rate scheme, it pays a percentage based on its total VAT-inclusive sales (exempt, zero rated and standard rated), so its VAT bill could be much higher.
- If the business is a 'limited cost business' it would have to pay the maximum flat rate percentage of 16.5% on its total VAT-inclusive sales, so its VAT bill could be much higher.

Chapter activities

Activity 3.1

Which one of the following businesses is more likely to benefit from joining the flat rate scheme for VAT accounting.

A business that makes mainly standard rated sales	☐
A business that makes mainly zero rated sales	☐
A business that makes mainly exempt sales	☐

Activity 3.2

A business submits its VAT Returns online and pays VAT to HMRC electronically by Direct Debit. The business is currently preparing its VAT return for the quarter ending 28 February 20X9.

The VAT return must be submitted to HMRC no later than ▼.

Assuming there are no weekends or bank holidays. HMRC will automatically collect payment from the business's bank account no earlier than ▼.

Picklist: 31 March 20X9, 7 April 20X9, 10 April 20X9, 30 April 20X9.

Activity 3.3

Show whether the following statements are true or false.

	TRUE	FALSE
Monthly returns can improve a business's cash flow, in particular when the business makes wholly or mainly zero-rated sales.	☐	☐
Monthly returns can improve a business's cash flow, in particular when the business makes wholly exempt sales.	☐	☐
When using the annual accounting scheme for VAT a business normally submits one VAT Return a year and makes payments of VAT four times a year.	☐	☐

Activity 3.4

Customers of a business are very slow payers and, in some cases, have not paid sales invoices for many months.

Which special accounting scheme for VAT is more likely beneficial to the business.

Flat rate scheme	☐
Cash accounting scheme	☐
Annual accounting scheme	☐

Activity 3.5

Show whether the following statements are true or false.

	TRUE	FALSE
Businesses can start on the annual accounting scheme if their estimated taxable turnover during the next tax year is not more than £1.35 million.	☐	☐
Businesses can start on the flat rate accounting scheme if their estimated taxable turnover during the next tax year is not more than £1.35 million.	☐	☐
A limited cost business is a business that typically has purchases that represent less than 2% of its sales turnover.	☐	☐

Activity 3.6

A business is preparing its VAT return for the quarter ended 30 June 20X2. The following transactions were recorded in the previous three months.

- Sales invoices £120,000 plus VAT.
- Payments received from customers £210,000 plus VAT.
- Purchases invoices £40,000 plus VAT.
- Payments made to suppliers £90,000 plus VAT.

Based only on the information above for the current VAT Return, is the business better off using the cash accounting scheme.

Picklist: Yes, No, Not possible to tell from the information.

Activity 3.7

A business submits its VAT Returns online and pays VAT due to HMRC electronically. It does not have a Direct Debit scheme in place with HMRC.

The business is currently preparing its VAT return for the quarter ending 28 February 20X9.

The VAT return must be submitted to HMRC and payment of any VAT due no later than

Picklist: 31 March 20X9, 7 April 20X9, 10 April 20X9, 30 April 20X9.

End of Task

4 VAT Penalties and VAT Errors

4.1 Introduction

This chapter will explain the following:

- The consequences of late submission and non-submission of VAT returns.
- The consequences of late payment or non-payment of VAT due.
- The consequences of failing to correct errors from previous VAT returns.
- Adjusting for errors or omissions from previous VAT returns.
- The soft-landing period (light touch approach) with regards to record keeping and filing penalties under Making Tax Digital (MTD).

AAT reference material is available during your exam which will include most of the information that is covered in this chapter. You are not required to have any knowledge of VAT penalty amounts and would not be required to calculate a VAT penalty in an exam task.

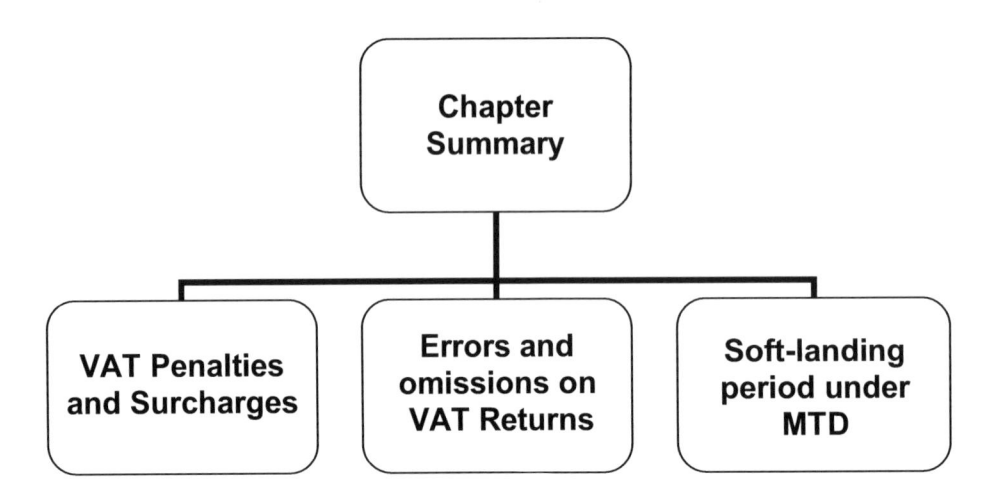

```
                    ┌──────────────┐
                    │   Chapter    │
                    │   Summary    │
                    └──────┬───────┘
            ┌──────────────┼──────────────┐
    ┌───────┴──────┐ ┌─────┴──────┐ ┌─────┴────────┐
    │ VAT Penalties│ │ Errors and │ │ Soft-landing │
    │ and Surcharges│ │ omissions on│ │ period under │
    │              │ │ VAT Returns │ │     MTD      │
    └──────────────┘ └────────────┘ └──────────────┘
```

4.2 Penalties for late VAT registration

Compulsory VAT registration is required by a business if either one of the following conditions are satisfied:

- Taxable turnover will be more than £85,000 in the next 30-day period (future turnover method), or
- Taxable turnover was more than £85,000 over the last 12-month period (historic turnover method).

If either one of the conditions are satisfied, the business has 30 days to notify HMRC it is required to be registered for VAT. HMRC may charge a civil penalty if a business fails to notify them on time that it should be registered for VAT. The amount of penalty charged will depend on the amount of VAT due and how late the business registered. HMRC will look closely at the circumstances of each case and if a reasonable excuse exists for late registration the business will not be liable to a civil penalty.

HMRC will also expect the business to pay any output VAT that should have been charged on its taxable sales, during the time the business should have been registered for VAT. The business has two choices in respect of output VAT that was not charged on sales invoices during this period, it can either:

- Treat sales invoices as VAT inclusive and absorb any output VAT which should have been charged to its customers, or
- Account for VAT as an addition to the charges already invoiced to its customers and attempt to recover the VAT amount from its customers. Customers are not legally obligated to pay this VAT amount, so this is an unlikely option for the business.

The business will be able to reclaim input VAT during the time it should have been registered for VAT.

4.3 Penalties for late submission of VAT Returns and payment of VAT due

A VAT registered business has a legal obligation to submit VAT returns and pay VAT owed to HMRC by the relevant due date. A default means a failure to fulfil an obligation, in this case failure to file a VAT return or pay VAT by the due date.

HMRC will record a 'default' for a business if:

- They have not received a VAT return by the due date, or
- Full payment for VAT on a VAT return has not been made by the due date.

The first default is dealt with by a warning known as a 'Surcharge Liability Notice'. This notice tells the business that if it submits its VAT return, or pays its VAT late again during the next 12-month period (the surcharge period), it may incur a surcharge:

- A surcharge means an additional charge (penalty).
- The business does not incur a surcharge (penalty) on its first default.
- The surcharge period is extended by a further 12 months, every time the business defaults during a surcharge period.

If a business does not submit a VAT return, HMRC has the powers to issue an estimated assessment of any VAT due, that they believe the business owes.

4.4 Penalties for deliberate or careless VAT errors

Non-careless errors

If a person discovers a non-careless VAT error (an error which is neither careless nor deliberate), HMRC expect that the person will take steps to correct it. If the person does not take steps to correct it, the inaccuracy will be treated as careless and liable to a penalty. Non-careless means that reasonable care was taken to avoid the error.

The majority of errors are treated as non-careless and so no penalty is normally due. People make mistakes and HMRC do not expect perfection when considering whether an error was careless, they are simply seeking to establish whether the person has taken the care and attention that would be expected from a person taking reasonable care.

Careless or deliberate errors

Careless or deliberate VAT errors discovered from previous VAT Returns are liable to a penalty. Telling HMRC about inaccuracies discovered as soon as the business is aware of them can help reduce the penalty (in some cases to zero).

The correction of deliberate errors from dishonest behaviour must always be reported to HMRC's VAT Error Correction Team, using form VAT652 'Notification of Errors in VAT Returns', or by writing to them directly. The business needs to provide a description of the inaccuracy, the full amount of the inaccuracy and how the inaccuracy arose. HMRC will then send a notice to confirm the amount calculated is correct and any interest or tax that is owed. Deliberate evasion of VAT is a criminal offence and could carry a possible prison sentence.

On a control visit to a business a VAT officer can examine VAT records to make sure that they are accurate and up to date. They also check that VAT amounts reclaimed from or paid to the government were correct. If HMRC carries out a VAT inspection and discovers VAT inaccuracies that have not been corrected or reported to HMRC at the time, it usually considers this to be careless and the business will be liable to a penalty. To avoid a penalty, the business must disclose full details of errors and omissions before HMRC begin making their enquiries.

4.5 Correcting errors from previous VAT Returns

A business may discover errors and omissions made in previous VAT Returns. The business would need to amend its VAT records and depending on the circumstances may account for VAT errors using one of two possible methods:

- **Method 1** Make an adjustment for previous errors on its current VAT Return.
- **Method 2** Separately declare previous errors to HMRC in writing and make no adjustment on its current VAT Return.

At the end of each VAT period, a business should calculate the net value of all errors and omissions it has discovered from previous VAT Returns submitted. The 'net value' means the amount of all output VAT errors and input VAT errors added together, it does not matter if the figure is positive or negative.

Method 1

If the net value of all errors and omissions is equal to or less than the 'error correction reporting threshold' (calculated below), then the amount may be corrected by simply making an adjustment on the current VAT Return (method 1). The business will not need to inform HMRC in writing (method 2).

The error correction reporting threshold is the greater of:

- £10,000, or
- 1% of the box 6 amount on the current VAT Return (this value subject to an upper limit of £50,000).

Box 6 is the total sales figure of the business excluding VAT on its current VAT Return.

There is an upper limit of £50,000 that would apply to any business that has total sales excluding VAT of £5 million or more on its current VAT Return (£5,000,000 ÷ 100% x 1% = £50,000 upper limit). This means that net error amounts discovered that exceed £50,000, then method 1 cannot be used and the business would have to inform HMRC in writing (method 2).

Even when the net error amount discovered is equal to or less than the 'error correction reporting threshold' a business may still decide to separately declare the amount to HMRC in writing (method 2).

Adjusting a current VAT return to correct net errors (method 1) and reclaiming input VAT from previous VAT Returns is subject to a strict 4-year time limit.

Method 2

A business must always report the following types of error in writing to HMRC:

- If the net value of all errors discovered is above the 'error reporting threshold'.
- Deliberate errors (that were made on purpose).

The correction of deliberate inaccuracies (from dishonest behaviour) must always be reported to HMRC's VAT Error Correction Team, using form VAT652 'Notification of Errors in VAT Returns', or by writing to them directly (method 2). The business needs to provide a description of the inaccuracy, the full amount of the inaccuracy and how the inaccuracy arose. HMRC will then send a notice to confirm the amount calculated is correct and any interest or tax that is owed. Deliberate evasion of VAT is a criminal offence and could carry a possible prison sentence.

Practice example

A business has discovered a deliberate error made in a previous VAT Return. The amount is £9,400. Total sales of £90,000 excluding VAT are included on box 6 of its current VAT Return.

Solution to practice example

The correction of deliberate inaccuracies must always be reported to HMRC's VAT Error Correction Team (method 2), regardless of the net error amount.

Practice example

A business has discovered non-deliberate errors that were made in a previous VAT Return. The net value of all errors discovered is £3,400 (output VAT £6,500 less input VAT £3,100). Total sales of £40,000 excluding VAT are included on box 6 of its current VAT Return.

Solution to practice example

The errors are non-deliberate so the error reporting threshold may apply.

The error reporting threshold is the greater of:

- £10,000, or
- 1% of £40,000 (box 6 amount) on the current VAT Return. £40,000 ÷ 100% x 1% = £400 (subject to an upper limit of £50,000).

The greater of the two amounts above is £10,000 (not £400). The net value of all errors is £3,400 and is below the threshold of £10,000, therefore method 1 can be used, and the errors corrected by making an adjustment on the current VAT Return. The business may still decide to separately declare the amounts to HMRC in writing and not make an adjustment on its current VAT Return (method 2).

The above example also demonstrates that £10,000 is the minimum threshold to report non-deliberate errors, regardless of the size of the business. Any net errors discovered that are equal to or below £10,000 allows method 1 to be used.

Practice example

A business has discovered non-deliberate errors that were made in a previous VAT Return. The net value of all errors discovered is £16,200 (output VAT £5,500 less input VAT £21,700). Total sales of £1,050,000 excluding VAT are included on box 6 of its current VAT Return.

Solution to practice example

The errors are non-deliberate so the error reporting threshold may apply.

The error reporting threshold is the greater of:

- £10,000, or
- 1% of £1,050,000 (box 6 amount) on the current VAT Return. £1,050,000 ÷ 100% x 1% = £10,500 (subject to an upper limit of £50,000).

The greater of the two amounts above is £10,500 (not £10,000). The net value of all errors is £16,200 and is above the reporting threshold of £10,500, therefore the business must separately declare these errors to HMRC and not make an adjustment on its current VAT Return (method 2).

The above example also demonstrates that a bigger business has a higher reporting threshold which can be greater than £10,000.

Practice example

A business has discovered non-deliberate errors that were made in a previous VAT Return. The net value of all errors is £26,100. Total sales of £5,600,000 excluding VAT are included on box 6 of its current VAT Return.

Solution to practice example

The errors are non-deliberate so the error reporting threshold may apply.

The error reporting threshold is the greater of:

- £10,000, or
- 1% of £5,600,000 (box 6 amount) on the current VAT Return. £5,600,000 ÷ 100% x 1% = £56,000 (subject to an upper limit of £50,000).

The greater of the two amounts above is £56,000 (not £10,000), however the threshold is subject to an upper limit of £50,000. The error reporting threshold is therefore £50,000. The net value of all errors is £26,100 and is below the threshold of £50,000, therefore method 1 can be used, and the net errors corrected by making an adjustment on the current VAT Return. The business may still decide to separately declare the amounts to HMRC in writing and not make an adjustment on its current VAT Return (method 2).

The above example also demonstrates that £50,000 is the maximum threshold to report non-deliberate errors, regardless of the size of the business. Any non-deliberate errors above £50,000 means that method 2 must be used and HMRC informed in writing.

4.6 Soft landing period for Making Tax Digital (MTD)

The soft-landing period (also called light touch approach) applies to record keeping and VAT filing penalties under MTD. HMRC will allow a period of time (a soft-landing period) for businesses to have in place digital links between all parts of their functional compatible software. Businesses will not be required to have full digital links between software programs until their first VAT Return period starting on or after 1 April 2021.

HMRC has been very clear that it wants businesses to continue to pay their VAT on time under MTD, so the light touch approach to late penalties does not extend to late filing of a VAT Return or the late or non-payment of VAT by the due date.

A 'digital link' is one where a transfer or exchange of data is made, or can be made, electronically between software programs, products or applications. That is without the involvement or need for manual intervention such as the copying over of information by hand or the manual transposition of data between 2 or more pieces of software.

Transferring data manually within or between different parts of a set of software programs, products or applications that make up functional compatible software is not acceptable under Making Tax Digital. However, during the soft-landing period, where a digital link has not been established between software programs, HMRC will accept the use of 'cut and paste' or 'copy and paste' as being a digital link for these VAT periods. The use of 'cut and paste' or 'copy and paste' would not normally constitute a digital link except during the soft-landing period.

4.7 Changes to VAT registration

A change in business details will usually necessitate a change in VAT registration details for example, a change in the trading name or address of the business. Other reasons can include a change to the business bank account details or to its main business activities, particularly if this means a significant change to the types of supply the business makes. Failure to notify HMRC of a change in VAT registration details within 30 days of the relevant change, may render the business liable to a penalty.

Chapter activities

Activity 4.1

Identify whether the following statements about the soft-landing period for record keeping and filing penalties under Making Tax Digital (MTD) are true or false.

	TRUE	FALSE
HMRC will allow a period of time for businesses to have in place digital links between all parts of their functional compatible software.	☐	☐
During the soft landing period, HMRC will not accept the use of 'cut and paste' or 'copy and paste' as being a digital link for VAT periods.	☐	☐
HMRC's soft landing period to penalties would include late payment of VAT by the business.	☐	☐

Activity 4.2

A business submits its VAT Return late and has submitted its previous two VAT Returns late to HMRC.

Which one of the following statements is most likely correct.

The business would incur a surcharge	☐
A Surcharge Liability Notice would be issued by HMRC	☐
A surcharge is only issued by HMRC if the businesses VAT return is late again	☐
No action would be taken by HMRC	☐

Activity 4.3

A business has discovered an error from a previous VAT Return.

Identify for each of the circumstances explained below, whether the error can be corrected by adjusting the current VAT Return of the business (method 1), or whether the business would need to make a separate declaration to HMRC's VAT Error Correction Team in writing about the mistake (method 2).

	Method 1	Method 2
A careless error made of £55,000. The total sales of the business included in box 6 of its current VAT Return is £6 million excluding VAT.	☐	☐
A deliberate error made of £24,000. The total sales of the business included in box 6 of its current VAT Return is £1.2 million excluding VAT.	☐	☐
A careless error made of £45,000. The total sales of the business included in box 6 of its current VAT Return is £6 million excluding VAT.	☐	☐

Activity 4.4

Identify whether the following statements are true or false.

	TRUE	FALSE
A Surcharge Liability Notice would be issued for late payment of VAT.	☐	☐
A business will pay a penalty every time it is issued with a Surcharge Liability Notice.	☐	☐
Deliberate VAT inaccuracies are a criminal offence and carry a possible prison sentence.	☐	☐

Activity 4.5

Identify whether the following circumstances will normally incur a penalty or not incur a penalty for a business.

	Penalty	No Penalty
Careless errors that are discovered from a previous VAT Return	☐	☐
Late VAT registration by a business	☐	☐
A business does not have full digital links between its software programs to submit its VAT Returns	☐	☐

End of Task

5 VAT Invoices and Tax Points

5.1 Introduction

This chapter will explain the following:

- The contents and form of a VAT invoice, simplified VAT invoice and e-invoice.
- Time limits for issuing VAT invoices, including the 14-day rule and 30-day rule.
- VAT rules for invoicing when prompt payment discounts (PPD) are offered to customers.
- How to determine the tax point of an invoice.

AAT reference material is available during your exam which will include most of the information that is covered in this chapter.

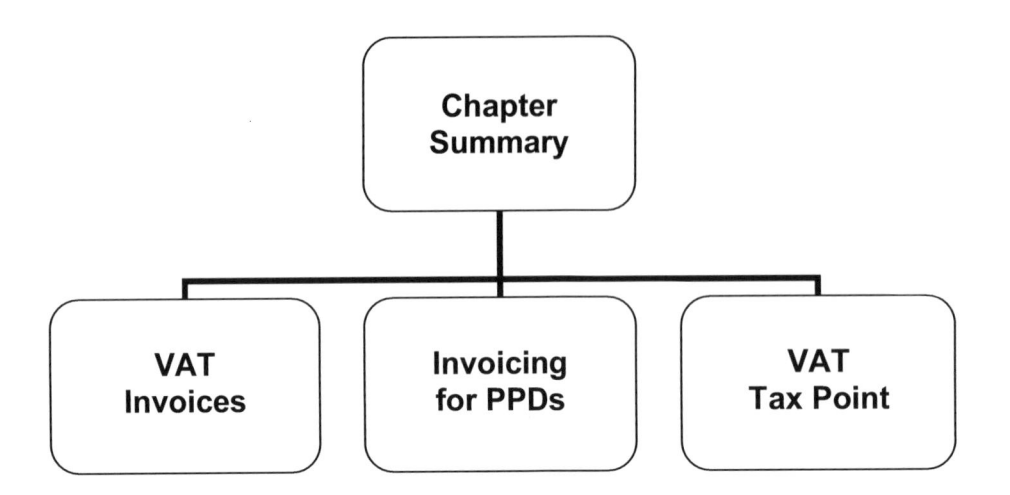

```
                    ┌─────────────┐
                    │   Chapter   │
                    │   Summary   │
                    └──────┬──────┘
            ┌──────────────┼──────────────┐
    ┌───────┴──────┐ ┌─────┴──────┐ ┌─────┴──────┐
    │     VAT      │ │ Invoicing  │ │    VAT     │
    │   Invoices   │ │  for PPDs  │ │ Tax Point  │
    └──────────────┘ └────────────┘ └────────────┘
```

5.2 VAT invoices

If a VAT registered business supplies taxable goods or services to another VAT registered business, it must give the customer a VAT invoice. A VAT registered customer must have a valid VAT invoice from the supplier to claim back the VAT they have paid on their taxable purchases.

A VAT registered business is not required to issue a VAT invoice to a business not registered for VAT, or to a member of the public (who is not VAT registered) but must do so if requested by the customer.

Only a VAT registered business must issue a VAT invoice, the invoice must show certain details about the supply of goods or services that were sold to the customer.

VAT invoice details:

- Unique invoice number that follows on from the last invoice.
- Business name, address and VAT number.
- Date and tax point (time of supply).
- Customer's name or trading name and address.
- Description of the goods or services supplied.
- Price per item, excluding VAT.
- Quantity of each type of item.
- Rate of any discount per item.
- Rate of VAT charged per item.
- Total amount excluding VAT.
- Total amount of VAT charged.
- Total amount including VAT.

A business does not need to issue a VAT invoice when the supply of goods or services are wholly exempt or zero-rated, in either case there is no VAT charged and therefore no VAT for the customer to reclaim. If mixed supplies are invoiced (mixture of standard rated, zero-rated supplies and exempt), the VAT invoice needs to make clear that no VAT has been charged on exempt or zero-rated items.

A VAT registered business must:

- Issue and keep valid VAT invoices (paper or electronic form).
- Keep copies of all sales invoices issued, even if cancelled or produced by mistake.
- Keep all purchase invoices for items it has purchased.

Electronic invoicing

The invoice details that must be shown on an electronic invoice is the same as a paper invoice. Electronic invoicing (e-invoicing) involves the transmission and storage of invoices by electronic (digital) means, the invoice is not printed or issued as a paper document. Electronic invoices are acceptable as valid VAT invoices if they are issued in a secure format such as a pdf file.

Simplified (less detailed) invoices

A simplified (less detailed) VAT invoice can be issued by a VAT registered business when the VAT inclusive amount of a sales transaction is less than £250. A simplified invoice cannot be issued if the sale includes any exempt supplies.

Simplified VAT invoice details:

- Business name, address and VAT number.
- Date and tax point (time of supply).
- Description of the goods or services.
- Rate of VAT charged per item.
- Total amount including VAT.

A simplified invoice is acceptable as a valid VAT invoice for a VAT registered customer to reclaim back the VAT they have paid. Compared to a normal VAT invoice, the information for a simplified invoice is much less detailed, it does not even need to show the total amount excluding VAT or amount of VAT charged.

What is not a valid VAT invoice

A VAT registered business cannot reclaim back VAT paid on purchases if using as proof of payment any of the below documents:

- Pro-forma invoices (see below).
- Invoices for only zero-rated or exempt supplies.
- Invoices that state 'this is not a VAT invoice'.
- Statements of account.
- Orders and delivery notes.
- Letters, emails, or other correspondence.

Pro-forma invoices

Pro-forma means as a 'matter of form or politeness' and this document cannot be used as a document to reclaim back VAT paid.

Characteristics of pro-forma invoices

- Issued before the goods or services are supplied.
- Like a 'sales quote' and not a valid VAT invoice.
- States that when payment is made a VAT invoice will be issued.
- Must be clearly marked 'THIS IS NOT A VAT INVOICE'.

Credit notes

A credit note is a negative or 'reverse' invoice that either cancels out an invoice completely or can be issued for less than the invoice amount due. Credit notes are used to reduce amounts owed by customers usually for goods returned or for prompt payment discounts. The document serves as official evidence of a reduction in the amount that a buyer owes the seller.

A credit note issued means an amount owed has been 'credited' to the customer's sales ledger account and the amount they owe has been reduced, the credit note serves as official evidence that this has happened.

If a VAT registered customer cannot wait for a credit note to be issued by a supplier, they can issue a 'debit note' themselves and send this to the supplier as official evidence they have 'debited' the purchases ledger account of the supplier and the amount owing to the supplier has been reduced.

A credit note issued by a seller or a debit note issued by a buyer are both valid VAT documents and VAT is accounted for in exactly the same way. Both documents must show the same details as a VAT invoice (unless a simplified invoice was issued).

5.3 Deadline to issue a VAT invoice

A VAT invoice must be issued within 30 days from the date of supply, or within 30 days from the date of payment if the customer has paid in advance. This strict time limit allows the customer to receive a valid VAT invoice in a timely manner and reclaim back VAT paid.

Practice example

A business dispatched goods on credit to a customer on 13 May 20X6. Payment has not been made by the customer.

When is the latest the business must issue a VAT invoice?

Solution to practice example

- The date of supply was 13 May 20X6.
- There was no advance payment before the 13 May 20X6.

The 30-day time limit to issue an invoice starts on the day the goods were sent. If you count 30 calendar days starting on the date 13 May 20X6, the invoice must be issued by the latest 11 June 20X6.

Practice example

A business dispatched goods to a customer on 13 May 20X6. The customer ordered and paid for the goods in advance on 2 May 20X6.

When is the latest the business must issue a VAT invoice?

Solution to practice example

- The date of supply was 13 May 20X6.
- Advance payment was made on 2 May 20X6 (earlier than supply).

The 30-day time limit to issue an invoice starts on the day the customer paid because payment was received earlier than supply. If you count 30 calendar days starting on the date 2 May 20X6, the invoice must be issued by the latest 31 May 20X6.

5.4 Rounding down pence on a VAT invoice

The VAT amount payable on a VAT invoice may be rounded down to the nearest whole penny, which means that any fraction of a penny can be ignored. So, if the VAT amount comes to 0.5 of one penny or more, the penny can be rounded down, rather than rounded up (if using mathematical principles).

Practice example

A manufacturer sells an item for £5.59 plus VAT.

Calculate the VAT amount that would be shown on an invoice?

Solution to practice example

VAT calculation:

- £5.59 x 20% VAT = £1.118 VAT amount.
- Round down any VAT to the nearest whole penny, the VAT amount is £1.11.
- The total VAT inclusive amount would be £5.59 + £1.11 = £6.70.

The concession to round down the penny is not available to retailers, so if the VAT comes to 0.5 of one penny or more for a retailer, the penny should be rounded up (same as if using mathematical principles). A retailer is a business that sells goods to the general public in relatively small quantities to each customer. A retailer could sell thousands of low-cost items and keep almost a full penny of VAT on each transaction. Manufacturers or wholesalers normally sell larger consignments of goods at much higher sales values for each transaction, so a penny difference is immaterial.

Practice example

A retailer sells an item for £5.59 plus VAT.

Calculate the VAT amount that would be shown on an invoice?

Solution to practice example

- £5.59 x 20% VAT = £1.118 VAT amount.
- Round up any VAT to the nearest whole penny because the 0.8 of one penny is a value of 0.5 or higher, the VAT amount is £1.12.
- The total VAT inclusive amount would be £5.59 + £1.12 = £6.71.

5.5 VAT accounting for discounts and goods returned

Goods returned

When goods are returned by a buyer, a seller has three options for VAT administration:
- Return the original invoice and issue a replacement invoice that shows the proper amount of VAT due.
- A credit note can be issued by the seller.
- A debit note can be issued by the buyer.

Discounts

In the exam you will need to understand how discounts are calculated and shown on an invoice or credit note. A discount means a deduction from the item price for goods or services sold.

Types of discount:
- A bulk discount is a discount available based on the quantity (volume) purchased.
- A trade discount is a discount available based on a customer's status or amount they spend.
- A prompt payment discount (PPD) is a discount available to incentivise a customer to pay their invoice early.

Bulk and trade discounts are deducted from the item price of the goods or services when the invoice is prepared, the net amount remaining after the discount is used to calculate any VAT payable. VAT is therefore calculated on the discounted price rather than the full price of goods or services.

Practice example

A business sells goods for £3,000 plus VAT. The customer is a regular customer and receives a 10% trade discount.

Calculate the net amount, VAT amount and total amount that is shown on an invoice?

Solution to practice example

Amounts shown on an invoice:
- Net amount excluding VAT is £3,000 less discount (10% of £3,000) = £2,700.
- VAT amount is £2,700 x 20% = £540.
- Total amount including VAT is £2,700 + £540 = £3,240.

A prompt payment discount (PPD) has uncertainty whether a customer will settle the invoice early and receive the PPD, or pay later and not receive the PPD.

A seller has three options for VAT administration:

- Issue the invoice with the PPD already deducted and issue an 'additional sales invoice' for the PPD amount if the customer pays the invoice late and is not entitled to it.
- Issue the invoice without the PPD deducted and issue a 'credit note' for the PPD amount if the customer pays the invoice early and is entitled to it.
- Issue the invoice with two amounts to pay, one amount to pay if the PPD is taken by the customer and the other amount to pay if the PPD is not taken by the customer.

Practice example

A business sells goods for £3,000 plus VAT. The business has offered a 2% discount if the customer settles the invoice within 7 days.

A seller has three options for VAT administration:

- Issue the invoice with the PPD deducted (total invoice amount £3,528) and issue an 'additional sales invoice' for the PPD amount (total invoice amount £72) if the customer pays the invoice late and is not entitled to it.
- Issue the invoice without the PPD deducted (total invoice amount £3,600) and issue a 'credit note' for the PPD amount (total credit note amount is £72) if the customer pays the invoice early and is entitled to it.
- Issue the invoice with two amounts to pay, one amount to pay if the PPD is taken by the customer (total invoice amount £3,528) and the other amount to pay if the PPD is not taken by the customer (total invoice amount £3,600).

Workings:

(1) Invoice amounts if PPD not taken:

- Total amount excluding VAT is £3,000.
- Total amount of VAT £3,000 x 20% = £600.
- Total amount including VAT is £3,000 + £600 = £3,600.

(2) Invoice amounts if PPD is taken:

- Total amount excluding VAT is £3,000 less discount (2% of £3,000) = £2,940.
- Total amount of VAT £2,940 x 20% = £588.
- Total amount including VAT is £2,940 + £588 = £3,528.

Amount of PPD (1) - (2) above:

- Total amount excluding VAT is £3,000 - £2,940 = £60.
- Total amount of VAT £600 - £588 = £12.
- Total amount including VAT is £3,600 - £3,528 = £72.

5.6 Tax points

A tax point is the date recognised to account for VAT payable on a VAT invoice. The tax point must be shown on a VAT invoice because this date determines the correct VAT Return period that VAT must be accounted for.

The basic tax point (the 'date of supply')

The basic tax point is always the date that goods were supplied or when services were performed (completed).

- For goods, supply is the date they were collected by the customer or sent to the customer.
- For goods installed at the customer's house, supply is the date the goods are completed and made available to the customer.
- For services, supply is the date the work was completed.

The basic tax point (date of supply) is normally the actual tax point that determines the correct VAT Return period that VAT should be accounted for, however the actual tax point can replace the basic tax point if:

- A VAT invoice has been issued within 14 days of the basic tax point (supply). The actual tax point will become the date of the invoice not the date of supply. This is known as the '14-day rule' for invoicing. If a VAT invoice is issued more than 14 days from the basic tax point, the 14-day rule is not applied.
- A payment is received in advance of supply and a VAT invoice has yet to be issued. The actual tax point will become the date payment was made. The payment date becomes the actual tax point not the date of supply. The '14-day rule' for invoicing does not apply in this case.
- A payment is received in advance of supply and a VAT invoice is issued in advance of supply. The actual tax point will be the earliest of either the payment date or the invoice date. The '14-day rule' for invoicing does not apply in this case.

Summary:

The actual tax point is the earliest of:

- Date of supply (basic tax point).
- Date of invoice.
- Date of payment.

The only exception to the rule above is when the basic tax point (supply) is the earliest of the three dates and the invoice is issued (sent) within 14 days after the basic tax point, in which case the invoice date becomes the actual tax point.

Practice example

A customer ordered goods on 14 December 20X8. Payment for the goods was made in advance by the customer on 14 December 20X8. The goods were collected by the customer on 7 January 20X9. The business invoiced the customer on 10 January 20X9.

What is the actual tax point to account for VAT in the correct VAT Return period?

Solution to practice example

- The date the goods were ordered is not relevant for tax points.
- Date of supply 7 January 20X9 (basic tax point).
- Date of invoice 10 January 20X9.
- Date of payment 14 December 20X8.

The earliest date shown above is the date of payment on 14 December 20X8 which is therefore the actual tax point. 14 December 20X8 determines the correct VAT Return period to account for the VAT.

Practice example

A customer ordered goods on 14 December 20X8. The goods were collected by the customer on 7 January 20X9. The business invoiced the customer for the goods on 15 December 20X8. Payment for the goods was made by the customer on 17 January 20X9.

What is the actual tax point to account for VAT in the correct VAT Return period?

Solution to practice example

- The date the goods were ordered is not relevant for tax points.
- Date of supply 7 January 20X9 (basic tax point).
- Date of invoice 15 December 20X8.
- Date of payment 17 January 20X9.

The earliest date shown above is the date of invoice on 15 December 20X8 which is therefore the actual tax point. 15 December 20X8 determines the correct VAT Return period to account for the VAT.

Practice example

A customer ordered goods on 14 December 20X8. The goods were sent to the customer on 18 December 20X8. The business invoiced the customer for the goods on 29 December 20X8. Payment was made by the customer on 7 January 20X9.

What is the actual tax point to account for VAT in the correct VAT Return period?

Solution to practice example

- The date the goods were ordered is not relevant for tax points.
- Date of supply 18 December 20X8 (basic tax point).
- Date of invoice 29 December 20X8.
- Date of payment 7 January 20X9.

The earliest date shown above is the date of supply (basic tax point) on 18 December 20X8. Whenever the basic tax point has been chosen, then check if the '14-day rule' for invoicing applies in this case. The invoice should be sent within 14 days of supply which is by the latest on 31 December 20X8 (within 14 days of 18 December 20X8). The invoice was sent within 14 days of supply, so the invoice date becomes the actual tax point. The invoice date on 29 December 20X8 determines the correct VAT Return period to account for the VAT.

Practice example

A customer ordered goods on 14 December 20X8. The goods were sent to the customer on 18 December 20X8. The business invoiced the customer for the goods on 3 January 20X9. Payment was made by the customer on 7 January 20X9.

What is the actual tax point to account for VAT in the correct VAT Return period?

Solution to practice example

- The date the goods were ordered is not relevant for tax points.
- Date of supply 18 December 20X8 (basic tax point).
- Date of invoice 3 January 20X9.
- Date of payment 7 January 20X9.

The earliest date shown above is the date of supply (basic tax point) on 18 December 20X8. Whenever the basic tax point has been chosen, then check if the '14-day rule' for invoicing applies in this case. The invoice should be sent within 14 days of supply which is by the latest on 31 December 20X8 (within 14 days of 18 December 20X8). The invoice was not sent within 14 days of supply, it was sent on 3 January 20X9. The date of supply (basic tax point) on 18 December 20X8 remains the actual tax point and determines the correct VAT Return period to account for the VAT.

Further aspects about tax points

To issue a VAT invoice, it must actually be sent to the customer for example, by post or email or handed to the customer for them to keep. A tax point cannot be created simply by preparing an invoice.

If a business has genuine commercial difficulties to invoice customers within 14 days of supply, they can contact HMRC and ask for permission to issue invoices later than 14 days and the invoice date can still become the actual tax point to replace the date of supply (basic tax point).

Deposits and further payments

Sometimes, a sales transaction can give rise to more than one tax point from the same transaction for example, if the customer pays a deposit in advance and then makes a further final payment.

Practice example

A customer ordered goods and paid a 40% deposit on 14 December 20X8. The goods were collected by the customer on 7 January 20X9. The business invoiced the customer in full for the goods on 18 January 20X9. Final payment for the goods was made by the customer on 21 January 20X9.

What is the actual tax point for the 40% deposit and final payment made by the customer?

Solution to practice example

Actual tax point for the 40% deposit:

- Date of supply 7 January 20X9.
- Date of invoice 18 January 20X9.
- Date of payment for the deposit 14 December 20X8.

The earliest date is the date of payment on 14 December 20X8 and is the actual tax point that determines the correct VAT Return period to account for the VAT on the 40% deposit paid.

Actual tax point for the 60% final payment:

- Date of supply 7 January 20X9.
- Date of invoice 18 January 20X9.
- Date of final payment 21 January 20X9.

The earliest date shown above is the date of supply (basic tax point) on 7 January 20X9. Whenever the basic tax point has been chosen, then check if the '14-day rule' for invoicing applies in this case. The invoice should be sent within 14 days of supply which is by the latest on 20 January 20X9 (within 14 days of 7 January 20X9). The invoice was sent within 14 days of supply, so the invoice date becomes the actual tax point. The invoice date on 18 January 20X9 determines the correct VAT Return period to account for the VAT on the 60% final payment.

Exceptions to the 'normal tax point rules'

- Credit (or debit) notes.
- VAT Cash Accounting Scheme.
- VAT Flat Rate Scheme.
- Services supplied on a continuous basis.
- Goods supplied on a sale or return basis.

The tax point rules are not used for the issue of credit notes (or debit notes). The issue of a credit note (or debit note) has no direct effect on a tax point, the tax point has already been established when the goods or services were supplied. What a credit note does is to permit the buyer to adjust their VAT previously accounted for on an invoice from an earlier tax point.

The tax point rules are not used for the VAT Cash Accounting Scheme, the actual tax point to account for VAT is always the date that payment is made.

The tax point rules are not used for the VAT Flat Rate Scheme, VAT payable is calculated as a percentage of total VAT inclusive turnover, the business cannot reclaim input VAT on its purchases.

The tax point rules are not used for services being supplied on a continuous basis over a period in excess of a month, as long as invoices are being issued regularly throughout the period. An actual tax point is created every time an invoice is issued, or a payment is made, whichever happens first. A business may issue invoices for a whole 12-month period but only if it is known that payments will be made regularly.

The tax point rules are not used for goods supplied to a buyer on a 'sale or return basis' because this arrangement is for the loan of goods, not for the sale of goods. The buyer only pays for the items if they sell them and can return any unsold items at the end of an agreed period.

Goods supplied on a sale or return basis is not a transfer of legal ownership, so when goods have passed to a buyer, no supply has taken place for VAT purposes. If no invoice is issued by the seller and no payment is made by the buyer, then VAT could be avoided for a long time because no actual tax point has arisen. Special rules therefore exist to determine the actual tax point for goods supplied on a sale or return basis.

The actual tax point is the earliest of:

- Any date that legal ownership of the goods transfers to the customer if goods have not been returned (this date is usually specified in the contract).
- 12 months from the date that the goods were sent to the customer.
- Any date the customer 'legally adopts' the goods, usually by written confirmation from the customer that they have accepted the goods.
- The date of payment for the goods by the customer.

The rules to determine an actual tax point (above) ensure that the maximum time limit for accounting for VAT is 12 months from the date that the goods were sent to the customer. The payment of a 'returnable deposit' by a customer (a deposit repayable if the goods are returned) is not considered a payment date.

Practice example

A business sent goods on a 'sale or return' basis to a client on 1 August 20X8. The contract specifies the client must return the goods within 6 months of being sent, otherwise legal ownership will transfer to the customer. The customer paid a returnable deposit for the goods on 30 July 20X8.

What is the actual tax point to account for VAT in the correct VAT Return period?

Solution to practice example

The actual tax point is the earliest of:

- The legal date that ownership transfers to the customer. The terms of the contract specify within 6 months of 1 August 20X8. A possible tax point could be on 31 January 20X9.
- Within 12 months from the date the goods were sent on 1 August 20X8. A possible tax point could be on 31 July 20X9.
- The date the customer 'adopts' the goods, there is no written acceptance at this point from the customer, but this could change in the future.
- The date of payment for the goods by the customer. No payment at this point from the customer other than a 'returnable deposit' which is not considered a payment date, but this could change in the future.

The current tax point will be 31 January 20X9 because it is the earliest date determined, unless the customer accepts the goods or pays for the goods before 31 January 20X9.

Chapter activities

Activity 5.1

Identify whether the following statements about simplified invoices are true or false.

	TRUE	FALSE
A simplified invoice can be issued only when the VAT inclusive amount of a sale is less than £25.	☐	☐
A simplified invoice must show the rate of VAT charged for each item sold.	☐	☐
A simple till receipt can be assumed to be acceptable as a simplified invoice for reclaiming VAT.	☐	☐

Activity 5.2

A business uses the VAT Cash Accounting Scheme. Goods were sent to a customer on 18 December 20X8. The business invoiced the customer for the goods on 3 January 20X9. Payment was made by the customer on 7 January 20X9.

Complete the following sentence.

The actual tax point for the sale of goods is ☐ ⬇

Picklist: 18 December 20X8, 3 January 20X9, 7 January 20X9.

Activity 5.3

A customer ordered goods and paid a 20% deposit in advance on 14 December 20X8. The goods were collected by the customer on 7 January 20X9. The business has not invoiced the customer and final payment for the goods has not been made.

Use drag and drop to identify the most likely tax point for the 20% deposit paid in advance and tax point for the final payment.

| 14 December 20X8 |
| 7 January 20X9 |
| 20 January 20X9 |

20% deposit	Final payment

Activity 5.4

Goods were collected by a customer on 7 June 20X9. The business invoiced the customer for the goods on 5 May 20X9. Payment for the goods was made by the customer on 7 May 20X9.

Identify the correct VAT Return when the transaction should be included.

VAT Return quarter ending 30 November 20X8	☐
VAT Return quarter ending 28 February 20X9	☐
VAT Return quarter ending 31 May 20X9	☐
VAT Return quarter ending 31 August 20X9	☐

Activity 5.5

Identify whether the following documents are a valid VAT invoice or not a valid VAT invoice.

	Valid VAT invoice	Not a valid VAT invoice
Pro-forma invoice	☐	☐
Invoice for only zero-rated or exempt supplies	☐	☐
Simplified invoice	☐	☐

Activity 5.6

A VAT registered business supplies to a customer, standard rated goods worth £200 and £25 worth of goods that are exempt for VAT purposes.

Complete the following sentence.

The business [⬇] issue a simplified VAT invoice.

Picklist: Can, Cannot.

Activity 5.7

Goods were sent to a customer on 18 December 20X2. The business invoiced the customer for the goods on 29 December 20X2. Payment was made by the customer on 7 January 20X3.

Complete the following sentence.

The actual tax point for the sale of goods is ▢

Picklist: 18 December 20X2, 29 December 20X2, 7 January 20X3.

End of Task

6 Reclaiming VAT

6.1 Introduction

This chapter will explain situations when it is not possible for a VAT registered business to reclaim some, or all of the input VAT it has paid on its purchases or expenses. Exam tasks may require you to calculate and adjust for the impact of disallowed amounts for VAT paid.

Situations when VAT paid cannot be reclaimed:

- Goods and services supplied to make wholly (100%) exempt supplies.
- Business goods and services supplied for private use, by an employee or business owner.
- Business entertaining of non-employees.
- New business motor cars, if there is private use by an employee or business owner.
- Business road fuel privately used by an employee or business owner.

This chapter will also explain the problem of recovering output VAT that has been paid on sales invoices, when the customer becomes a bad debt.

AAT reference material is available during your exam which will include most of the information that is covered in this chapter.

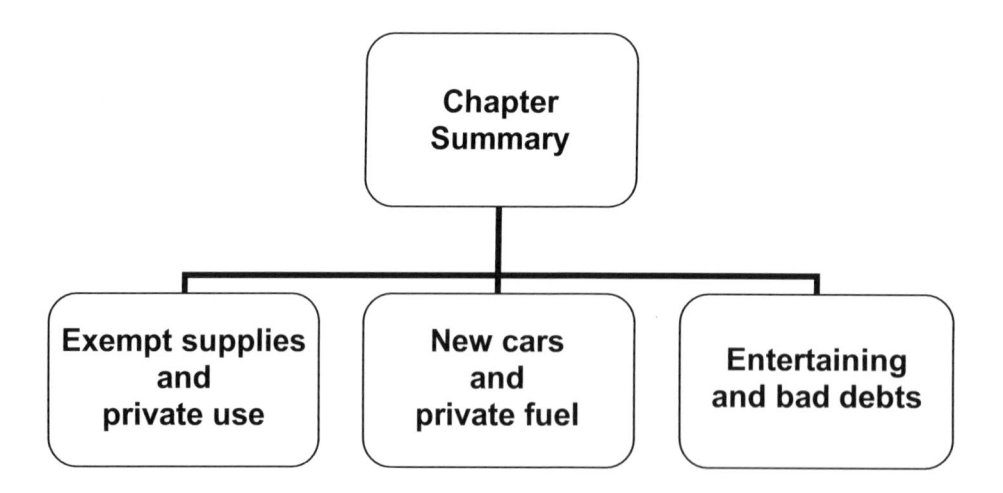

Chapter Summary
- Exempt supplies and private use
- New cars and private fuel
- Entertaining and bad debts

6.2 Exempt (non-taxable) supplies

A business that makes wholly (100%) exempt supplies

Exempt supplies are non-taxable sales, which means that VAT is not charged on the selling price for these type of goods or services. A business that makes wholly (100%) exempt supplies cannot register for VAT, therefore input VAT paid on standard-rated purchases and expenses that relate to exempt sales, cannot be reclaimed.

A business that makes partly exempt supplies

A VAT registered business is partly exempt, if it sells both taxable supplies (standard-rated or zero-rated sales) and non-taxable supplies (exempt sales).

- The business would charge output VAT on its taxable supplies and reclaim input VAT paid on its standard-rated purchases and expenses, that relate to taxable supplies.
- The business would not charge output VAT on its exempt (non-taxable) supplies and normally cannot reclaim input VAT paid on its standard-rated purchases and expenses that relate to exempt supplies, unless this amount of input VAT is below the 'de minimis' amount.

De minimis means 'insignificant or trivial things'.

- If the amount of input tax that relates to exempt supplies is less than (or equal to) the 'de minimis' amount, then it can be reclaimed by the business.
- If the amount of input tax that relates to exempt supplies is more than the 'de minimis' amount, then it cannot be reclaimed by the business.

An exam task would explain whether input tax that relates to exempt supplies is above or below the de minimis amount, you are not required to know the de minimis amount, only the rule.

6.3 Private use

No input VAT can be reclaimed on goods and services supplied for private use by an employee or business owner. Examples of a personal or 'non-business' nature include motor fuel used for private purposes, private phone calls and goods or other benefits provided by the business, to enjoy for private consumption.

If the expenditure has a mixed business and non-business (private) nature, the input VAT paid should be apportioned on a fair and reasonable basis. For example, if the business pays all phone bills and 30% of the cost of all calls made by the business owner were for private purposes, then 30% of the input VAT paid on phone bills would be disallowed and not reclaimed by the business. 70% of the input VAT paid on phone bills would be reclaimed by the business as these calls were made for business purposes.

6.4 New cars and fuel

New cars

A business is not normally able to reclaim input VAT it has paid on the purchase price of a new car, unless the car is used wholly (100%) for business purposes. The car must not be available for private use and this may be specified as evidence in employee contracts. Private use incudes any non-business use of the car and would include an employee or business owner, using the car to travel between home and work.

The business may be able to reclaim all the VAT paid if the new car is mainly used:

- As a taxi.
- For driving instruction.
- For self-drive hire.

If input VAT paid on a new car is not reclaimed by the business because of private use, the future sale of the car will be a non-taxable (exempt) supply for VAT purposes and the business would not charge output VAT on the sale. If input VAT paid on a new car is reclaimed by the business because of 100% business use, the future sale of the car will be a taxable (standard-rated) supply for VAT purposes and the business would charge output VAT on the sale.

Leasing a car

If a business leases a car, it can usually claim back 50% of the input VAT paid if there is private use. Normally all the VAT paid is reclaimed, if the car is used wholly (100%) for business purposes.

Other types of motor vehicle (other than cars)

A VAT-registered business can normally reclaim the input VAT paid when it buys a commercial vehicle such as a motor bike, van, lorry, forklift truck or tractor. Input VAT is normally reclaimed by the business and therefore the future sale of the vehicle would be a taxable (standard-rated) supply for VAT purposes and the business would charge output VAT on the sale.

Motor vehicle expenses

Whenever a car or any other type of vehicle is used for business purposes, the business can reclaim all input VAT paid on vehicle repairs and maintenance, even if the vehicle is used for private use.

A business can reclaim all input VAT paid on fuel such as petrol or diesel, for commercial vehicles such as a lorry, motorcycle or van, even if the vehicle is used for private use.

A business can reclaim all input VAT paid on fuel for cars, if the car is used wholly (100%) for business purposes. The business must be able to prove that fuel used was strictly for business purposes and no private journeys were undertaken. This is usually impossible to prove unless the business is a taxi firm or a driving school.

In most cases there is private use for cars by employees and business owners and HMRC allow a business to choose one of three ways to account for the input VAT paid on car fuel:

1. Reclaim input VAT paid that relates only to the fuel used for business miles travelled and disallow input VAT paid for private miles travelled. Detailed records of business and private mileage must be kept for each car as evidence.
2. Do not reclaim any input VAT paid on fuel for each car. If this option is chosen then detailed records of business and private miles driven do not need to be kept, but the business will be unable to reclaim input VAT paid on fuel for all vehicles it owns, including vans, lorries etc, so this can be a poor option for cash-flow. It is a useful option if the miles driven on cars are low, the cost of fuel used is mainly for private miles and the business does not own any other vehicles.
3. Use HMRC published fuel scale charges to pay back some VAT for the cost of private fuel consumed on each car. This option allows the business to reclaim all input VAT paid on fuel and detailed records of business and private miles driven do not need to be kept for each car.

Fuel scale charges simplify VAT accounting. The fuel scale charge amount for each car depends on the cars CO_2 emissions figure, an exam task will always give the value of any fuel scale charge whenever relevant. A fuel scale charge is equivalent to a sales invoice issued for the taxable supply of private (non-business) fuel used by an employee or business owner, therefore output VAT is payable on each VAT Return.

- A fuel scale charge is a fixed charge added to output VAT on the VAT return.
- The business reclaims all input VAT paid on fuel on the VAT return.
- The two amounts offset and so less VAT on fuel is reclaimed overall.

Practice example

A VAT registered business paid £380.70 including VAT on fuel used for a business car driven by an employee. Detailed mileage records show that the employee used the car 60% for business use and 40% for private use. The relevant HMRC fuel scale charge for the relevant VAT period is £180 including VAT. The business needs to choose one of three methods to account for the input VAT paid on fuel.

1. Reclaim input VAT paid that relates only to the fuel used for business miles travelled and disallow input VAT paid for private miles travelled.

- £380.70 including VAT was paid for fuel used on the car, input VAT paid on fuel was £380.70 ÷ 120% x 20% VAT = £63.45 input VAT paid.
- 40% of fuel is for private use and not reclaimed by the business, £63.45 input VAT ÷ 100% x 40% = £25.38 input VAT paid that is not reclaimed.
- 60% of fuel is for business use and is reclaimed by the business, £63.45 input VAT ÷ 100% x 60% = £38.07 input VAT paid that is reclaimed.
- The business will enter £38.07 as input VAT reclaimed on its VAT Return.

2. Do not reclaim any input VAT paid on fuel for the car.

- £63.45 input VAT paid on fuel will not be reclaimed by the business.
- The business will enter £0 as input VAT reclaimed on its VAT Return.

If the business chooses this option, it will be unable to reclaim input VAT paid on fuel for all vehicles it owns including vans, lorries etc.

3. Use fuel scale charges to pay back some VAT for the cost of private fuel consumed on the car.

- The relevant HMRC fuel scale charge for the relevant VAT period is £180 including VAT. £180 ÷ 120% x 20% VAT = £30.00 output VAT.
- The business will enter £30.00 output VAT payable on its VAT Return.
- The business will enter £63.45 input VAT reclaimed on its VAT Return.
- The net VAT reclaimed from HMRC would be £33.45 (£63.45 - £30.00).

Summary of cash-flow position

- Option 1, £38.07 VAT reclaimed.
- Option 2, £0 VAT reclaimed.
- Option 3, £33.45 VAT reclaimed.

The business would be better off in this situation using option 1 to maximise its reclaim of VAT paid on fuel.

6.5 Business and employee entertainment

Business entertainment is any form of free or subsidised entertainment or hospitality to 'non-employees'. Examples include hotel accommodation, food and drink, tickets to events, participation in lunches, dinners, parties, sporting activities or similar business gatherings. A non-employee is a person who is not an employee of the business such as a customer, supplier or guest of an employee.

- Input VAT paid for business entertainment, normally cannot be reclaimed by a business, however one exception is entertaining overseas customers (customers not from the UK or Isle of Man).
- Input VAT paid for employee entertainment, normally can be recovered by a business, but not for any guests of employees because a guest is a 'non-employee'. VAT can be reclaimed on most employee expenses such as entertainment, travel and subsistence.

Summary

Reclaim input VAT paid for entertaining:

- Overseas customers.
- Employees.

Do not reclaim input VAT paid for entertaining:

- UK or Isle of Man customers.
- UK, Isle of Man or overseas suppliers.
- Guests of employees, customers or suppliers.

When the nature of entertainment is for a mixture of the above persons, the business can only reclaim input VAT paid on the proportion of expenditure that relates to employees and overseas customers only. For example, if 40% of those who attended were overseas customers and employees, then 40% of the input VAT can be reclaimed on the VAT Return. The other 60% of the input VAT is disallowed and not reclaimed on the VAT Return.

6.6 Bad debts

If a VAT registered business makes a supply (sale) to a customer and does not get paid, it can claim bad debt relief and recover any output VAT it has paid on sales invoices that are irrecoverable.

Bad debt relief cannot be claimed until ALL of the following conditions are met:

- The business has accounted for and paid output VAT on the supplies (sales) it made to the customer.
- The business has written off the debt in its VAT account and as an expense in its profit or loss account.
- The value of supplies (sales) was not more than the customary or normal selling price for such goods or services and ownership has passed to the customer.
- The debt has not been sold to a factoring company. A factoring company buys outstanding invoices from a business, normally for slow paying customers.
- The debt is more than six months old and less than four years and six months old, from the later of the date of supply, or when payment of the invoice was due.

One exception when a business does not have to claim bad debt relief is for a business that uses the Cash Accounting Scheme for VAT. Output VAT from a sales invoice would only be accounted for when the customer has paid, therefore bad debt relief is automatic and unnecessary to claim, because no output VAT is payable unless the customer pays.

Chapter activities

Activity 6.1

Identify whether the following statements are true or false.

	TRUE	FALSE
A VAT registered business can normally reclaim VAT on the purchase price of a new car, if the car is used for self drive hire by its customers.	☐	☐
A VAT registered business can normally reclaim VAT on the purchase of commercial vehicles, such as lorries or vans.	☐	☐
A business can normally reclaim all VAT it pays on private fuel used, for company vehicles driven by employees.	☐	☐

Activity 6.2

A business is partly exempt for VAT purposes and has input VAT which it wants to reclaim for its current VAT return. Input VAT paid in connection with taxable and exempt supplies include the following:

	Input VAT
Standard Rated Supplies	£3,701
Zero Rated Supplies	£2,444
Exempt Supplies	£8,772

Input tax that relates to exempt supplies is more than the de minimis limit.

Complete the following sentence.

The amount of input VAT that can be reclaimed by the business is [   ]

Picklist: All of it, Some of it, None of it.

Activity 6.3

A business held an annual party and invited its customers, suppliers, employees and any guests.

Complete the following sentence.

The amount of input VAT that can be reclaimed by the business is [ ]

Picklist: All of it, Some of it, None of it.

Activity 6.4

A business is preparing its VAT return and needs to calculate VAT reclaimed on fuel used by an employee, that has driven a business car for private use.

- Total input VAT paid on fuel for the car in the relevant VAT period was £16.67.
- The fuel scale charge for the car for the relevant VAT period is £150 including VAT.

Calculate the net amount of VAT payable or reclaimed by the business, if it uses fuel scale charges to account for VAT on private fuel. Do not use a minus sign or brackets. Round your answer to two decimal places.

£ [ ]

Activity 6.5

A business operates no special accounting schemes for VAT. It supplied standard rated goods to a customer and invoiced them for £2,000 plus VAT on 2 February 20X2. The invoice was due to be paid by 4 March 20X2. All conditions for claiming bad debt relief have been met.

Identify which VAT Return gives the earliest opportunity for the business to claim bad debt relief.

VAT period ending 31 January 20X2	☐
VAT period ending 30 April 20X2	☐
VAT period ending 31 July 20X2	☐
VAT period ending 31 October 20X2	☐

Activity 6.6

Identify for each of the following types of expenditure, whether a business can normally reclaim all input VAT or reclaim no input VAT.

	Reclaim ALL input VAT	Reclaim NO input VAT
Staff entertainment expenditure paid for by the business.	☐	☐
Repairs and maintenance costs for a business van.	☐	☐
The purchase of a new car by the business, that will be driven sometimes privately by an employee.	☐	☐

Activity 6.7

Identify whether each of the following statements are true or false.

	TRUE	FALSE
A business can normally recover input VAT in connection with employee travel and subsistence.	☐	☐
Input VAT paid for entertaining UK customers, can normally be reclaimed by a VAT registered business.	☐	☐
A business entertains staff and one guest only for each member of staff at a Christmas party, all input VAT is reclaimable.	☐	☐

End of Task

Overseas Transactions

7.1 Introduction

This chapter will explain the following:

- Calculating and accounting for VAT on imports and exports for non-EU countries.
- Calculating and accounting for VAT on acquisitions and despatches for EU countries.
- How to invoice and account for VAT in circumstances where 'reverse charges' are applicable.

The EU means the European Union and may also be referred to as the EC (European Community). Exam tasks will not require you to know which countries are EU or non-EU member states and this information will always be provided whenever relevant to an exam task.

It is worth noting there is changes to the VAT rules and procedures for transactions between the UK and EU member states from 1 January 2021, due to Brexit, currently these new changes are beyond the scope of your syllabus.

AAT reference material is available during your exam which will include most of the information that is covered in this chapter.

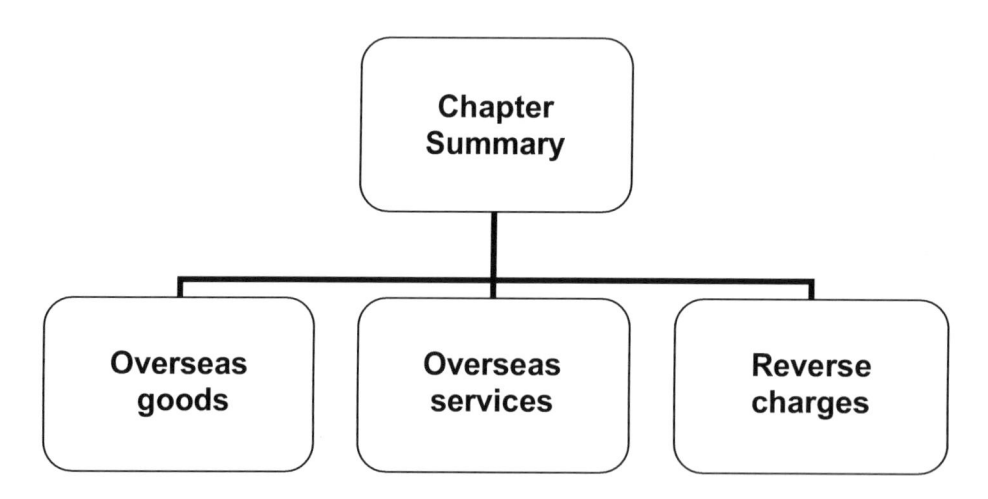

```
                    ┌──────────────┐
                    │   Chapter    │
                    │   Summary    │
                    └──────┬───────┘
            ┌──────────────┼──────────────┐
      ┌─────┴─────┐  ┌─────┴─────┐  ┌─────┴─────┐
      │ Overseas  │  │ Overseas  │  │  Reverse  │
      │   goods   │  │ services  │  │  charges  │
      └───────────┘  └───────────┘  └───────────┘
```

7.2 Overseas goods

A UK VAT registered business that supplies (sells) goods to, or receives (purchases) goods from an EU member state or country outside the EU, must apply certain VAT rules and procedures to account for such transactions.

The 'place of supply' rules determine the location where goods have been supplied and therefore the amount of VAT due (if any) and who needs to account for it. The following rules normally apply to a VAT registered business located in the UK, with no alternative locations elsewhere in the EU or outside the EU.

Sale of goods overseas by a UK VAT registered business

- The term exports describes the sale of goods overseas to a country outside the EU. **Exports are normally zero-rated supplies.** The business must follow strict rules, obtain and keep any necessary evidence of the transaction and obey all laws.
- The term dispatches describes the sale of goods overseas to a country which is an EU member. **Dispatches are normally zero-rated supplies.** Provided the customer is a VAT registered business in their own EU member country. If dispatches are made to a business or person, who is not registered for VAT in their own EU member country, the UK business must normally charge VAT at the same VAT rate that would apply if the type of goods had been sold in the UK.

Purchase of goods from overseas by a UK VAT registered business

The term imports describes the cost of goods purchased and any related costs (insurance and delivery) from a supplier located outside the EU. VAT is normally payable on all purchases of goods from a non-EU country at the same VAT rate that would apply if the type of goods had been purchased in the UK. The business must tell HMRC about any goods that it imports from a non-EU country and pay any VAT due.

VAT is normally charged on non-EU goods, at the point the goods arrive at UK borders, unless the UK business has a direct debit scheme in place with HMRC, it must pay any VAT due before customs can release the goods. A UK VAT registered business can reclaim any input VAT paid on imported goods.

The term acquisitions describes the cost of goods purchased and any related costs (insurance and delivery) from a supplier located in an EU country. If a UK VAT registered business buys goods from another VAT registered business located in an EU country, the supply is normally zero-rated by the seller. However, the UK business must normally account for VAT reverse charges on their VAT Return (see later).

Summary

Overseas Sales	**Dispatches** (EU members)	Zero rated sale
	Exports (non-EU members)	Zero rated sale
Overseas Purchases	**Acquisitions** (EU members)	Buyer accounts for reverse charges (no VAT is charged by the seller)
	Imports (non-EU members)	VAT charged at the point of entry in the UK

7.3 Overseas services

A UK VAT registered business that perform their services overseas, or receive services performed from a business located in an EU member state or country outside the EU, must apply certain VAT rules and procedures to account for such transactions.

The 'place of supply' rules determine the location where services have been supplied and therefore the amount of VAT due (if any) and who needs to account for it. The following rules normally apply to a VAT registered business located in the UK, with no alternative locations elsewhere in the EU or outside the EU.

Sale of services overseas by a UK VAT registered business

If a business is located in the UK and the place of supply of its services is performed in the UK, it must charge VAT if the services are a taxable supply, regardless of where the customer is located.

If a business is located in the UK and the place of supply of its services is overseas (rather than in the UK), then different place of supply rules exist depending on whether the services are to another business B2B (business-to-business) or to a consumer B2C (business-to-consumer). A consumer is a private individual (or unregistered business) and the services are performed therefore for non-business use.

- If the customer is a business customer (B2B) the place of supply is where the customer is located (overseas) and the supply is normally 'outside the scope' of UK VAT. This means no VAT is charged and the transaction is not accounted for on a VAT Return
- If the customer is a non-business customer (B2C) the place of supply is where the supplier is (the UK), regardless of where the customer is located. The UK business must normally charge VAT at the same VAT rate that would apply if the type of service had been performed in the UK.

Purchases of services from overseas by a UK VAT registered business

If a UK VAT registered business buys services overseas from another VAT registered business located in an EU country, the seller would normally zero-rate the sale. However, the UK business must normally account for VAT reverse charges (similar to acquisitions of goods from the EU) on their VAT Return (see later).

If a UK business buys services overseas from a non-EU country, then normally no UK VAT is charged (unlike imported goods).

Summary

Sale of services overseas	Services performed overseas for another business (B2B)	Outside the scope of VAT
	Services performed overseas for private or non-business customers (B2C)	VAT charged at the same rate that would apply, as if services were supplied in the UK
Purchase of services overseas	EU member	Buyer (UK business) accounts for VAT reverse charges and no VAT is charged by the seller
	Non-EU member	UK VAT is not charged

7.4 How to invoice and account for VAT reverse charges

A reverse charge for invoicing is a way of accounting for VAT when a UK VAT registered business buys goods and services from another VAT registered business, located in an EU country.

Reverse charges can apply to:

- VAT on goods purchased (acquisitions) and any services directly related to those goods, such as delivery and insurance costs, from another VAT registered business located in an EU member state.
- VAT due on the supply of services performed by another VAT registered business located in an EU member state.

A reverse charge is a mechanism for accounting for VAT and one of the reasons why an invoice may not charge VAT. Normally a seller charges VAT on its supplies (sales) and reclaims VAT on its purchases. A reverse charge deviates from this rule, instead the seller does not charge VAT on the sales invoice and the customer (buyer) accounts for both the sellers output tax and their own input tax at the same time on their own VAT return. This is called a 'reverse charge' because normally the seller not the buyer accounts for any output tax on the sale.

Example of how reverse charges work

A UK VAT registered business buys goods or services from another VAT registered business, located in an EU country.

The business located in the EU country will send a sales invoice to the UK buyer without VAT charged (VAT rate as 0%) and usually with a note indicating that a 'reverse charge' applies and a sentence that explains why there is no VAT charged on the invoice. The invoice normally includes the UK buyers VAT number. The seller does not account for any VAT because the sales invoice is zero-rated by the seller (VAT rate as 0%).

The UK buyer pays the net amount due on the invoice (VAT rate as 0%). Assuming the type of goods or services are standard rated in the UK, the UK buyer will manually calculate VAT at 20% on the invoice as a reverse charge. The buyer will then report the VAT amount as both input VAT and output VAT on their own VAT return. The two VAT entries on the buyers VAT return are for the same amount, so they cancel each other out and no VAT is actually paid to HMRC.

Reverse charges have no effect on the sellers or the buyers cash-flow because no VAT is actually paid by either party.

This example also works in reverse, so if a UK VAT registered business supplies goods to a VAT registered business located in an EU country, the UK seller 'zero rates' the sale and the EU buyer would account for VAT reverse charges in their own country.

Chapter activities

Activity 7.1

Complete the following sentence.

A reverse charge is when a [_____] does not charge VAT on the invoice and the [_____] would account for the input tax and output tax on their VAT return.

Picklist: Seller, Buyer.

Activity 7.2

Identify whether the following statements about reverse charges are true or false.

	TRUE	FALSE
Under the reverse charge mechanism, a seller will send an invoice to the buyer without VAT charged.	☐	☐
The seller would report the same VAT amount as both input VAT and output VAT on their VAT Return.	☐	☐
Reverse charges have no effect on the sellers or buyers cash flow.	☐	☐

Activity 7.3

Complete the following sentence.

When a UK VAT registered business supplies services to an overseas business, if the place of supply is overseas the sale is usually [⬇]

Picklist: Zero-rated, Standard-rated, Exempt, Outside the scope of VAT.

Activity 7.4

Complete the following sentences.

[⬇] are goods supplied to overseas customers outside the EU.

[⬇] are goods supplied to overseas customers in an EU member state.

Picklist: Imports, Acquisitions, Exports, Dispatches.

End of Task

8 VAT Returns

8.1 Introduction

This chapter will explain the following:

- How to complete VAT returns from accounting information provided.
- How to make appropriate adjustments on a current VAT return for errors discovered from a previous VAT return.

Exam tasks will expect you to communicate VAT information such as the amount of VAT due to HMRC or reclaimed from HMRC, due dates for payment of VAT due and the effects of special VAT schemes on VAT payment or recovery.

AAT reference material is available during your exam which will include most of the information that is covered in this chapter.

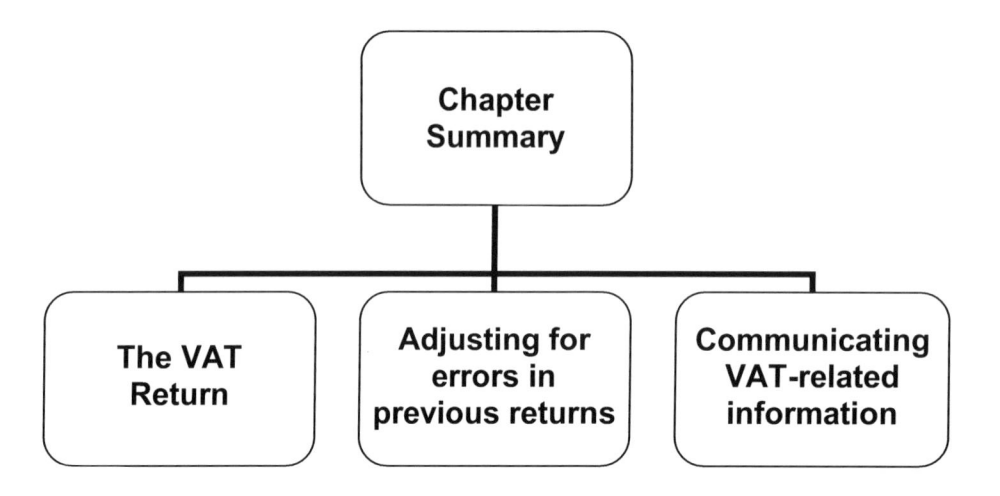

```
                    ┌──────────────┐
                    │   Chapter    │
                    │   Summary    │
                    └──────┬───────┘
           ┌───────────────┼───────────────┐
    ┌──────┴─────┐  ┌──────┴──────┐  ┌─────┴────────┐
    │  The VAT   │  │ Adjusting   │  │ Communicating│
    │   Return   │  │ for errors  │  │  VAT-related │
    │            │  │ in previous │  │  information │
    │            │  │   returns   │  │              │
    └────────────┘  └─────────────┘  └──────────────┘
```

8.2 Terminology for VAT returns

Virtually all VAT-registered businesses are required by law to submit their VAT returns online and pay their VAT due electronically. Common terminology used for VAT Returns include:

Output VAT

This is the VAT payable from the sale of goods or services. These sales are known as outputs. Output VAT is VAT charged and collected from customers by a VAT registered business.

Input VAT

This is the VAT reclaimed on the purchase of goods and services. These purchases are known as inputs. Input VAT is normally recovered by a VAT registered business.

Net VAT paid or reclaimed

A VAT Return records output VAT payable and input VAT reclaimed by the business. If output VAT is greater than input VAT, the difference is owed (due) to HMRC. If output VAT is less than input VAT, the difference is repaid by HMRC to the business.

VAT period

The top of a VAT return shows the relevant period to account for VAT for example, a quarterly VAT return may cover the period from 1 January 20X8 to 31 March 20X8.

Tax point

There are VAT rules for working out the time that goods or services were supplied (the 'tax point rules'). The tax point must be shown on a VAT invoice and it determines the correct VAT return period to account for each transaction.

Imports

Goods and related costs purchased from suppliers outside the EU. A VAT registered business in the UK can reclaim any VAT that it pays on these goods as input VAT.

Acquisitions

Goods and related costs from suppliers located inside the EU. If the goods would normally be standard rated in the UK, then a UK VAT registered business normally has to account for the sellers output VAT (reverse charge) and recover their own input VAT. Reverse charges have no effect on the sellers or the buyers cash-flow because no VAT is actually paid by either party.

Exports

Goods sold outside the EU. These supplies are normally zero-rated.

Dispatches

Goods sold inside the EU. These supplies are normally zero-rated.

8.3 The VAT Return

Exam tasks will expect you to identify and extract any relevant income, expenditure and VAT figures from accounting records such as day books, or ledgers accounts such as the sales and sales returns accounts, purchases and purchases returns accounts, cash and petty cash accounts and the VAT account.

Day books keep a record of a business's past transactions and documents such as invoices, credit notes and bank receipts and payments. At the end of each period the day books are totalled, and the summarised totals posted to the general ledger accounts using the double entry system.

The sales, sales returns, purchases and purchases returns accounts record transactions excluding VAT, since the VAT amount for each transaction would be posted to a VAT account.

Example of a VAT Return

A VAT Return will be provided for you to complete as an exam task and the proforma will be similar to the example shown below.

On-line VAT Return for period ended 31 December 20X1	
Please note: Enter values in pounds sterling, including pence, for example 1000.00, except where indicated.	
VAT due in this period on sales and other outputs (Box 1)	
VAT due in this period on acquisitions from other EC member states (Box 2)	
Total VAT due (the sum of boxes 1 and 2) (Box 3)	
VAT reclaimed in the period on purchases and other inputs (including acquisitions from the EC) (Box 4)	
Net VAT to be paid to HM Revenue & Customs or reclaimed by you (difference between boxes 3 and 4) (Box 5)	
Total value of sales and all other outputs excluding any VAT. Include your Box 8 figure. (Box 6)	Enter values in whole pounds only
Total value of purchases and all other inputs excluding any VAT. Include your Box 9 figure. (Box 7)	Enter values in whole pounds only
Total value of all supplies of goods and related costs, excluding any VAT, to other EC member states (Box 8)	Enter values in whole pounds only
Total value of all acquisitions of goods and related costs, excluding any VAT, to other EC member states (Box 9)	Enter values in whole pounds only

Recording information on a VAT Return

- Box 1 to Box 5 would be VAT amounts entered in pounds and pence.
- Box 6 to Box 9 would be sales and purchases amounts (excluding VAT) entered in whole pounds only.
- When preparing a VAT Return, the exam task will accept as a correct answer, amounts rounded up or rounded down, either answer is acceptable to gain full marks in the task.

Box 1 - VAT due in this period on sales and other outputs

Increase output VAT payable in this box:

- Output VAT on standard rated sales to UK customers.
- Output VAT on fuel scale charges.
- Reverse charges (20% VAT) on the 'supply of services' (not goods) purchased from an EC member state. Include the same amount of VAT also in Box 4.
- Underpaid output VAT from errors discovered in a previous VAT Return.

Decrease output VAT payable in this box:

- Output VAT on standard rated credit notes issued to UK customers (or debit notes issued from UK customers) because of sales returns and prompt payment discounts.
- Overpaid output VAT from errors discovered in a previous VAT Return.

Box 2 - VAT due in this period on acquisitions from other EC member states

Increase output VAT payable in this box:

- Reverse charges (20% VAT) on acquisitions (goods) from an EC member state. Include the same amount of VAT in Box 4.

Box 3 - Total VAT due (the sum of Boxes 1 and 2)

- This is calculated automatically by the online return.

Box 4 - VAT reclaimed in the period on purchases and other inputs

Increase input VAT reclaimed in this box:

- Input VAT reclaimed on UK standard rated purchases.
- Input VAT reclaimed on standard rated imports from countries outside the EC.
- Reverse charges (20% VAT) on the 'supply of services' (not goods) purchased from an EC member state. Include the same amount of VAT in Box 1.
- Reverse charges (20% VAT) on acquisitions (goods) from an EC member state. Include the same amount of VAT in Box 2.
- Underclaimed input VAT from errors discovered in a previous VAT Return.
- Output VAT claimed as bad debt relief.

Decrease input VAT reclaimed in this box:

- Input VAT on standard rated credit notes issued from UK suppliers (or debit notes issued to UK suppliers) because of purchases returns and prompt payment discounts.
- Overclaimed input VAT from errors discovered in a previous VAT Return.

Box 5 - Net VAT to be paid to HMRC or reclaimed from HMRC

- Box 3 (total output VAT due) minus Box 4 (total input VAT reclaimed).
- This is calculated automatically by the online return.

Box 6 - Total value of sales and all other outputs, excluding any VAT

- **Add:** Sales to UK customers, excluding VAT (standard rated, zero rated and exempt supplies).
- **Less:** Sales credit notes (or debit notes), excluding VAT (standard rated, zero rated and exempt supplies).
- **Add:** Sales (exports) to outside the EC (zero rated supplies).
- **Add:** Sales (dispatches and related costs) to the EC (zero rated supplies). Include the same amount in Box 8.
- **Add:** Fuel scale charges, excluding VAT.

Box 7 - Total value of purchases and all other inputs, excluding any VAT

- **Add:** Purchases from UK suppliers, excluding VAT (standard rated, zero rated and exempt supplies).
- **Less:** Purchase credit notes (or debit notes), excluding VAT (standard rated, zero rated and exempt supplies).
- **Add:** Purchases (imports) from outside the EC, excluding VAT.
- **Add:** Purchases (acquisitions and related costs) from the EC, excluding VAT. Also include the same amount in Box 9.
- **Add:** Purchases of services performed from the EC and outside the EC, excluding VAT.

Box 8 - Total value of all supplies of goods and related costs, excluding any VAT, to other EC member states

- **Add:** Sales (dispatches) to the EC (zero rated supplies). Include the same amount in Box 6.

Box 9 - Total value of all acquisitions of goods and related costs, excluding any VAT, to other EC member states

- **Add:** Purchases (acquisitions including delivery costs) from the EC, excluding VAT. Also include the same amount in Box 7.

8.4 Accounting for overseas transactions on a VAT Return

Sale of goods overseas

- EC members (dispatches and related costs). Sale of goods are zero-rated, enter sale amounts excluding VAT in Box 6 and Box 8.
- Non-EC members (exports). Sale of goods are zero-rated, enter sale amounts excluding VAT in Box 6 only.

Purchase of goods from overseas

- EC members (acquisitions and related costs). Enter 20% VAT (reverse charge) in Box 2 and Box 4 if the goods are standard rated in the UK. Enter purchase amounts excluding VAT in Box 7 and Box 9.
- Non-EC members (imports). Enter VAT in Box 4 if the goods are standard rated in the UK. Enter purchase amounts excluding VAT in Box 7.

Sale of services overseas

- The sale of services performed overseas (to an EC or non-EC country) is normally outside the scope of VAT which means the transaction is not accounted for on a VAT Return.

Purchase of services from overseas

- EC members. Enter 20% VAT (reverse charge) in Box 1 and Box 4 if the services are standard rated in the UK. Enter purchase amounts excluding VAT in Box 7.
- Non-EC members. Enter purchase amounts excluding VAT in Box 7 only. No UK VAT applies because the services are not performed in the UK.

8.5 Accounting for errors discovered from a previous VAT Return

The net value of all non-deliberate errors discovered from a previous VAT Return, can be corrected on the current VAT Return, if the net value is equal to or less than the error correction reporting threshold. The net value of errors is the amount of output VAT and input VAT (underpaid or overpaid) all added together (positive or negative).

Box 1 (if net value of errors is output VAT only)

- Increase this box for underpaid output VAT from errors discovered in a previous VAT Return.
- Decrease this box for overpaid output VAT from errors discovered in a previous VAT Return.

Box 4 (if net value of errors is input VAT only)

- Increase this box for underclaimed input VAT from errors discovered in a previous VAT Return.
- Decrease this box for overclaimed input VAT from errors discovered in a previous VAT Return.

Box 1 or Box 4 (if net value of errors is a mixture of output VAT and input VAT)

When both input VAT and output VAT errors are discovered from a previous VAT Return in the same exercise, the net value of all errors will be used to adjust the VAT Return and either Box 1 or Box 4 is adjusted as appropriate.

Example 1

If a business discovered that it did not account for output VAT to HMRC of £56.00 on a supply made in the past and did not account for £90.00 input VAT reclaimed on a purchase, then it should add £34.00 to Box 4 on the current VAT Return (£34.00 more input VAT than output VAT).

Example 2

If a business discovered that it did not account for output VAT to HMRC of £85.00 on a supply made in the past and did not account for £14.00 input VAT reclaimed on a purchase, then it should add £71.00 to Box 1 on the current VAT Return (£71.00 more output VAT than input VAT).

8.6 Accounting for bad debts on a VAT Return

If a VAT registered business makes a supply (sale) to a customer and does not get paid, it can claim bad debt relief and recover any output VAT it has paid on the sales invoices that are irrecoverable. Bad debt relief cannot be claimed until certain conditions have been met. The amount of output VAT is added to Box 4 of the VAT Return when accounting for bad debt relief.

8.7 Accounting for fuel scale charges on a VAT Return

Fuel scale charges simplify VAT accounting for private fuel. The fuel scale charge amount for each car depends on the cars CO2 emissions figure, an exam task will always give the value of any fuel scale charge whenever relevant. A fuel scale charge is equivalent to a sales invoice issued for the taxable supply of private (non-business) fuel used by an employee or business owner, therefore output VAT is payable on each VAT Return.

- A fixed charge is added to output VAT payable (Box 1) on the VAT return.
- The business reclaims all input VAT paid on fuel (Box 4) on the VAT return.
- The two amounts offset (Box 1 and Box 4) and so less VAT is reclaimed on fuel overall by the business.

Practice example

A VAT registered business paid £380.70 including VAT on fuel used for a business car driven by an employee. There is private use of the car by the employee. The relevant HMRC fuel scale charge for the relevant VAT period is £180 including VAT.

Solution to practice example

The fuel scale charge for the relevant VAT period is £180 including VAT. £180 ÷ 120% x 20% VAT = £30.00 output VAT.

- The business will enter £30.00 output VAT payable (Box 1) on its VAT Return.
- The business will enter £150 (£180 - £30) as a sale excluding VAT (Box 6) on its VAT Return.

£380.70 including VAT was paid for fuel used on the car, input VAT paid on fuel was £380.70 ÷ 120% x 20% VAT = £63.45 input VAT paid.

- The business will enter £63.45 input VAT reclaimed (Box 4) on its VAT Return.

8.8 Accounting for partly exempt supplies on a VAT Return

A VAT registered business is partly exempt, if it sells both taxable supplies (standard-rated or zero-rated sales) and non-taxable supplies (exempt sales).

- The business would charge output VAT on its taxable supplies and reclaim input VAT paid on its standard-rated purchases and expenses, that relate to taxable supplies.
- The business would not charge output VAT on its exempt (non-taxable) supplies and normally cannot reclaim input VAT paid on its standard-rated purchases and expenses that relate to exempt supplies, unless this amount of input VAT is below the 'de minimis' amount.

De minimis means 'insignificant or trivial things'.

- If the amount of input tax that relates to exempt supplies is less than (or equal to) the 'de minimis' amount, then it can be reclaimed by the business.
- If the amount of input tax that relates to exempt supplies is more than the 'de minimis' amount, then it cannot be reclaimed by the business.

An exam task would explain whether input tax that relates to exempt supplies is above or below the de minimis amount, you are not required to know the de minimis amount, only the rule.

8.9 Accounting for input VAT disallowed on a VAT Return

Any amount of input VAT disallowed would be excluded from Box 4 of the VAT return.

Examples of input VAT disallowed

- Business goods and services supplied for private use.
- Business entertaining of non-employees.
- New business motor cars, when there is private use.
- Business car fuel when there is private use and fuel scale charges not used.

Chapter activities

Activity 8.1

A business has voluntarily registered for VAT but has not registered for Making Tax Digital. You need to prepare all the figures for completion of its on-line VAT Return for the period ended 31 December.

The following accounts have been extracted from the ledgers.

Sales account

Date	Details	Debit £	Date	Details	Credit £
31/12	Balance c/d	134,313.59	1/10-31/12	Sales day book - UK sales	121,922.92
			1/10-31/12	Cash book - UK sales	12,390.67
	Total	134,313.59		Total	134,313.59

Purchases account

Date	Details	Debit £	Date	Details	Credit £
1/10-31/12	Purchases day book - UK purchases	34,922.88	31/12	Balance c/d	44,904.48
1/10-31/12	Purchases day book - EU acquisitions	5,000.00			
1/10-31/12	Cash book - UK purchases	4,981.60			
	Total	44,904.48		Total	44,904.48

VAT account

Date	Details	Debit £	Date	Details	Credit £
1/10-31/12	Purchases day book - UK purchases	6,984.57	1/10-31/12	Sales day book - UK sales	24,384.58
1/10-31/12	Cash book - UK purchases	996.32	1/10-31/12	Cash book - UK sales	2,478.13

You are told that all EU acquisitions were standard rated goods.

(a) Enter the relevant figures into the on-line VAT Return for the period ended 31 December.
Do not leave any box blank.

On-line VAT Return for period ended 31 December	
Please note: Enter values in pounds sterling, including pence, for example 1000.00, except where indicated.	
VAT due in this period on sales and other outputs (Box 1)	
VAT due in this period on acquisitions from other EC member states (Box 2)	
Total VAT due (the sum of boxes 1 and 2) (Box 3)	**Calculated value**
VAT reclaimed in the period on purchases and other inputs (including acquisitions from the EC) (Box 4)	
Net VAT to be paid to HM Revenue & Customs or reclaimed by you (difference between boxes 3 and 4) (Box 5)	**Calculated value**
Total value of sales and all other outputs excluding any VAT. Include your Box 8 figure. (Box 6)	Enter values in whole pounds only
Total value of purchases and all other inputs excluding any VAT. Include your Box 9 figure. (Box 7)	Enter values in whole pounds only
Total value of all supplies of goods and related costs, excluding any VAT, to other EC member states (Box 8)	Enter values in whole pounds only
Total value of all acquisitions of goods and related costs, excluding any VAT, to other EC member states (Box 9)	Enter values in whole pounds only

(b) Calculate the values that will be shown on-line when you submit the VAT Return for the following boxes. If a repayment is due, use a minus sign in Box 5. Enter the values in pounds sterling, including pence.

Total VAT due (the sum of boxes 1 and 2) (Box 3)

Net VAT to be paid to HM Revenue & Customs or reclaimed by you (difference between boxes 3 and 4) (Box 5)

Activity 8.2

A business has voluntarily registered for VAT but has not registered for Making Tax Digital. You need to prepare all the figures for completion of its on-line VAT Return for the period ended 31 May.

The following information has been extracted from the day books and accounting records of the business for the period ended 31 May.

Day book summaries	Goods £	VAT £	Total £
Sales	47,999.22	9,194.84	57,194.06
Sales returns	550.00	110.00	660.00
Purchases	7,862.47	1,572.49	9,434.96
Purchase returns	295.60	59.12	354.72
Discounts allowed	575.99	115.20	691.19
Discounts received	23.58	4.72	28.30

Further information	Net £	VAT £	Total £
Motor vehicle expenses	2,090.13	418.02	2,508.15

- Motor vehicle expenses are not processed through the purchases day book and all input VAT is recoverable.
- Cash sales of £22,400 were made, excluding VAT at 20%. The net amount was posted to the cash sales account for the period.
- All purchases are on credit terms.
- There were no overseas transactions.

(a) Enter the relevant figures into the on-line VAT Return for the period ended 31 May.
Do not leave any box blank.

On-line VAT Return for period ended 31 May	
Please note: Enter values in pounds sterling, including pence, for example 1000.00, except where indicated.	
VAT due in this period on sales and other outputs (Box 1)	
VAT due in this period on acquisitions from other EC member states (Box 2)	
Total VAT due (the sum of boxes 1 and 2) (Box 3)	**Calculated value**
VAT reclaimed in the period on purchases and other inputs (including acquisitions from the EC) (Box 4)	
Net VAT to be paid to HM Revenue & Customs or reclaimed by you (difference between boxes 3 and 4) (Box 5)	**Calculated value**
Total value of sales and all other outputs excluding any VAT. Include your Box 8 figure. (Box 6)	Enter values in whole pounds only
Total value of purchases and all other inputs excluding any VAT. Include your Box 9 figure. (Box 7)	Enter values in whole pounds only
Total value of all supplies of goods and related costs, excluding any VAT, to other EC member states (Box 8)	Enter values in whole pounds only
Total value of all acquisitions of goods and related costs, excluding any VAT, to other EC member states (Box 9)	Enter values in whole pounds only

(b) Calculate the values that will be shown on-line when you submit the VAT Return for the following boxes. If a repayment is due, use a minus sign in Box 5. Enter the values in pounds sterling, including pence.

Total VAT due (the sum of boxes 1 and 2) (Box 3)

Net VAT to be paid to HM Revenue & Customs or reclaimed by you (difference between boxes 3 and 4) (Box 5)

Activity 8.3

A business has voluntarily registered for VAT but has not registered for Making Tax Digital. You need to prepare all the figures for completion of its on-line VAT Return for the period ended 30 April.

The following accounts have been extracted from the ledgers.

Sales account

Date	Details	Debit £	Date	Details	Credit £
30/4	Balance c/d	108,663.09	1/2-30/4	Sales day book - UK sales	90,972.12
			1/2-30/4	Sales day book - EU Dispatches	12,390.00
			1/2-30/4	Cash book - UK sales	5,300.97
	Total	108,663.09		Total	108,663.09

Purchases account

Date	Details	Debit £	Date	Details	Credit £
1/2-30/4	Purchases day book - UK purchases	109,922.82	30/4	Balance c/d	117,004.60
1/2-30/4	Cash book - UK purchases	7,081.78			
	Total	117,004.60		Total	117,004.60

VAT account

Date	Details	Debit £	Date	Details	Credit £
1/2-30/4	Purchases day book - UK purchases	21,984.56	1/2-30/4	Sales day book - UK sales	18,194.42
1/2-30/4	Cash book - UK purchases	1,416.35	1/2-30/4	Cash book - UK sales	1,060.19

You are told that all EU Dispatches were zero-rated goods.

(a) Enter the relevant figures into the on-line VAT Return for the period ended 30 April.
Do not leave any box blank.

On-line VAT Return for period ended 30 April	
Please note: Enter values in pounds sterling, including pence, for example 1000.00, except where indicated.	
VAT due in this period on sales and other outputs (Box 1)	
VAT due in this period on acquisitions from other EC member states (Box 2)	
Total VAT due (the sum of boxes 1 and 2) (Box 3)	**Calculated value**
VAT reclaimed in the period on purchases and other inputs (including acquisitions from the EC) (Box 4)	
Net VAT to be paid to HM Revenue & Customs or reclaimed by you (difference between boxes 3 and 4) (Box 5)	**Calculated value**
Total value of sales and all other outputs excluding any VAT. Include your Box 8 figure. (Box 6)	Enter values in whole pounds only
Total value of purchases and all other inputs excluding any VAT. Include your Box 9 figure. (Box 7)	Enter values in whole pounds only
Total value of all supplies of goods and related costs, excluding any VAT, to other EC member states (Box 8)	Enter values in whole pounds only
Total value of all acquisitions of goods and related costs, excluding any VAT, to other EC member states (Box 9)	Enter values in whole pounds only

(b) Calculate the values that will be shown on-line when you submit the VAT Return for the following boxes. If a repayment is due, use a minus sign in Box 5. Enter the values in pounds sterling, including pence.

Total VAT due (the sum of boxes 1 and 2) (Box 3)

Net VAT to be paid to HM Revenue & Customs or reclaimed by you (difference between boxes 3 and 4) (Box 5)

Activity 8.4

You work for an accountancy practice and have just submitted an on-line VAT Return for a client who is the owner of a business. The business pays HMRC any VAT due by Direct Debit. Today's date is Wednesday 24 June, there are no bank holidays in June or July.

The following information has been submitted on-line for the clients quarterly VAT Return.

On-line VAT Return for period ended 31 May	
VAT due in this period on sales and other outputs (Box 1)	11150.71
VAT due in this period on acquisitions from other EC member states (Box 2)	1000.00
Total VAT due (the sum of boxes 1 and 2) (Box 3)	**Calculated value**
VAT reclaimed in the period on purchases and other inputs (including acquisitions from the EC) (Box 4)	8464.57
Net VAT to be paid to HM Revenue & Customs or reclaimed by you (difference between boxes 3 and 4) (Box 5)	**Calculated value**

Complete the following e-mail to the owner of the business.

To: Owner of the business
From: Accounting Technician
Date: Wednesday 24 June
Subject: Completed VAT Return

Please be advised that the VAT Return for the period ended 31 May has been completed.

The amount of VAT [▼] will be £ [ ]

Picklist: Payable, Reclaimable.

Please allow sufficient funds to permit HMRC to direct debit your account on [▼]

Picklist: Tuesday 30 June, Tuesday 7 July, Friday 10 July.

Kind regards,

Accounting Technician

Activity 8.5

You work for an accountancy practice and will be submitting an on-line VAT Return for a client who is the owner of a business. The business does not have a Direct Debit scheme in place with HMRC. Today's date is Wednesday 29 July.

The VAT Return is for the period ended 30 June. The following information has been provided by the client for this return period.

- Standard rated sales £26,000 plus 20% VAT.
- Zero rated sales £6,000.
- The business joined the flat rate scheme for VAT three years ago.
- The flat rate percentage is 11% for the business.

The client has also queried how much their business turnover needs to be for them to continue using the flat rate scheme for VAT.

Complete the following e-mail to the owner of the business.

To: Owner of the business
From: Accounting Technician
Date: Wednesday 29 July
Subject: VAT Return using the flat rate scheme for VAT

Please be advised that the VAT Return for the period ended 30 June will be completed today.

The amount of VAT [   ] will be £ [   ]

Picklist: Payable, Reclaimable.

Please ensure the amount of any VAT due is paid by [   ]

Picklist: Friday 31 July, Friday 7 August, Wednesday 12 August.

The business can use the flat rate scheme for VAT if its VAT [   ] taxable turnover is less than £150,000 per year, the business could simplify its VAT accounting by registering on the Flat Rate Scheme and calculating VAT payments as a percentage of its total VAT [   ] turnover.

Picklist: Inclusive, Exclusive.

Once on the flat rate scheme, the business can continue to use it until its total business income exceeds [   ].

Picklist: £150,000, £230,000.

Kind regards,

Accounting Technician

Activity 8.6

You need to prepare selected figures for a business's VAT Return for the period ended 31 December. The following accounts have been extracted from the ledgers.

Sales account

Date	Details	Debit £	Date	Details	Credit £
1/10-31/12	Sales returns day book - UK	655.55	1/10-31/12	Sales day book - UK	51,522.90
31/12	Balance c/d	53,367.35	1/10-31/12	Cash book - UK sales	2,500.00
	Total	54,022.90		Total	54,022.90

VAT account

Date	Details	Debit £	Date	Details	Credit £
1/10-31/12	Sales returns day book - UK sales	131.11	1/10-31/12	Purchases returns day book - UK purchases	710.24
1/10-31/12	Purchases day book - UK purchases	8,304.56	1/10-31/12	Sales day book - UK sales	10,304.58
			1/10-31/12	Cash book - UK sales	500.00

The following transactions have not been accounted for:

- During the relevant VAT period private fuel was paid by the business for an employee driving a business car. The business reclaims all VAT on the cost of fuel and pays the relevant fuel scale charge. The relevant HMRC fuel scale charge for the VAT period is £240 including VAT.
- A sales invoice for £2,400 excluding VAT has been omitted from the accounting records shown above, the goods sold were zero-rated supplies.

(a) Calculate the figure that should be included in box 1 of the VAT Return, once any necessary corrections have been made to the ledger accounts. Enter your figure in pounds sterling, including pence.

£ ☐

(b) Calculate the figure that should be included in box 4 of the VAT Return, once any necessary corrections have been made to the ledger accounts. Enter your figure in pounds sterling, including pence.

£ ☐

(c) Calculate the figure that should be included in box 6 of the VAT Return, once any necessary corrections have been made to the ledger accounts. Enter your figure in whole pounds only.

£ ☐

Activity 8.7

You need to prepare selected figures for a business's VAT Return for the period ended 30 April. The following accounts have been extracted from the ledgers.

Sales account

Date	Details	Debit £	Date	Details	Credit £
30/4	Balance c/d	69,713.09	1/2-30/4	Sales day book - UK sales	55,972.12
			1/2-30/4	Sales day book - Exports to outside the EC	10,390.00
			1/2-30/4	Cash book - UK sales	3,350.97
	Total	69,713.09		Total	69,713.09

Purchases account

Date	Details	Debit £	Date	Details	Credit £
1/2-30/4	Purchases day book - UK purchases	39,922.82	30/4	Balance c/d	45,004.60
1/2-30/4	Cash book - UK purchases	5,081.78			
	Total	45,004.60		Total	45,004.60

VAT account

Date	Details	Debit £	Date	Details	Credit £
1/2-30/4	Purchases day book - UK purchases	7,984.56	1/2-30/4	Sales day book - UK sales	11,194.42
1/2-30/4	Cash book - UK purchases	1,016.35	1/2-30/4	Cash book - UK sales	670.19

Two invoices were omitted from a previous VAT Return.
- A standard rated sales invoice for £2,800 excluding VAT.
- A standard rated purchase invoice for £450 excluding VAT.

The business is able to correct the above invoices on the current VAT Return.

(a) Calculate the net value of all errors used to adjust the current VAT Return. Enter your figure in pounds sterling, including pence.

£ _____

(b) Calculate the figure that should be included in box 1 of the VAT Return, once any necessary corrections have been made to the ledger accounts. Enter your figure in pounds sterling, including pence.

£ _____

(c) Calculate the figure that should be included in box 4 of the VAT Return, once any necessary corrections have been made to the ledger accounts. Enter your figure in pounds sterling, including pence.

£ ☐

Activity 8.8

A business made a non-careless and non-deliberate error on a previous VAT Return.

- VAT of £56 on a purchase invoice from a UK supplier was omitted in the accounting records.
- VAT of £8 on a credit note from a UK supplier was duplicated in the accounting records.

The business is allowed to correct the net error on its current VAT Return.

Which one of the following corrections should the business make in Box 4 of its current VAT Return.

Add £64	☐
Add £48	☐
Deduct £64	☐
Deduct £48	☐

End of Task

Solutions to Chapter Activities

Solutions to chapter 1 activities

Activity 1.1 - Solution

Show whether the following statements about VAT are true or false.

	TRUE	FALSE
Output VAT is charged by a VAT registered business, on its sales made to both other businesses and ordinary consumers.	✓	
Input tax can normally be reclaimed back by a VAT registered business from HMRC.	✓	
Business outputs are the total value of sales and all other outputs including VAT.		✓

The third statement is false because business outputs are the total value of sales and all other outputs excluding (not including) VAT.

Activity 1.2 - Solution

Calculate the VAT on the following sales figures that are excluding VAT. The VAT rate is 20%. Show your numerical answers to TWO decimal places.

(i) £27.75

£5.55.

Using percentages, the amount is (£27.75 ÷ 100% x 20%) = £5.55.

(ii) £388.65

£77.73.

Using percentages, the amount is (£388.65 ÷ 100% x 20%) = £77.73.

(iii) £49.95

£9.99.

Using percentages, the amount is (£49.95 ÷ 100% x 20%) = £9.99.

Activity 1.3 - Solution

Calculate the VAT on the following sales figures that are including VAT. The VAT rate is 20%. Show your numerical answers to TWO decimal places.

(i) £45.60

£7.60.

Using percentages, the amount is (£45.60 ÷ 120% x 20%) = £7.60.

(ii) £401.94

£66.99.

Using percentages, the amount is (£401.94 ÷ 120% x 20%) = £66.99.

(iii) £107.40

£17.90.

Using percentages, the amount is (£107.40 ÷ 120% x 20%) = £17.90.

Activity 1.4 - Solution

A business has total purchases of £3,605.22 including VAT. The rate of VAT is 20%. Show all numerical answers to TWO decimal places.

The net purchases figure is.

£3004.35.

Using percentages, the amount is (£3,605.22 ÷ 120% x 100%) = £3,004.35. Alternatively, if the VAT figure is known, £3,605.22 - £600.87 = £3,004.35.

The VAT figure is.

£600.87.

Using percentages, the amount is (£3,605.22 ÷ 120% x 20%) = £600.87.

Activity 1.5 - Solution

Show whether the following statements about VAT are true or false.

	TRUE	FALSE
Value added tax (VAT) is a tax charged on the sale of most goods or services in the UK by a VAT-registered business.	✓	☐
Inputs are the total value of purchases and all other inputs including VAT.	☐	✓
HMRC is the government department responsible for operating the VAT system.	✓	☐

The second statement is false because business inputs are the total value of purchases and all other inputs excluding (not including) VAT.

Activity 1.6 - Solution

Identify what type of software is a digital tool that acts as the middleman between other applications and the HMRC portal for submitting VAT returns online.

Bridging software	✓
MTD-compatible software	☐
Electronic invoicing	☐
Accounting software	☐

A wholesaler buys a good for £3,000 plus VAT of £600 and then sells the good to a retailer for £7,000 plus VAT of £1,400. The retailer sells the good for £15,000 plus VAT of £3,000 to a non-VAT registered business. Both the wholesaler and retailer are a VAT registered business. The rate of VAT is 20%.

Activity 1.7 - Solution

Calculate the cost to each of the parties for the £3,000 VAT received by HMRC. If your answer is zero, enter '0'.

Cost to the wholesaler

£0.

Cost to the retailer

£0.

Cost to the non-VAT registered business

£3,000.

VAT is collected and administered by a VAT registered business, but it is ultimately suffered by the general public or a non-VAT registered business who is not able to reclaim back VAT they have suffered.

Activity 1.8 - Solution

A business recorded an invoice sent to a customer showing VAT of £1,270, the correct VAT amount that should have been recorded was £1,207. Currently the business's VAT account shows output tax of £6,230 and input tax of £1,380.

Identify which of the following figures will be shown in the business's VAT account when the error has been corrected.

Input tax £1,317	☐
Input tax £1,443	☐
Output tax £6,293	☐
Output tax £6,167	✓

VAT on sales invoices to customers would increase output tax payable by the business. Output VAT was increased by £1,270, but the correct VAT amount should have increased output VAT by £1,207. Output tax currently payable of £6,230, must be reduced by £63 (£1,270 - £1,207). £6,230 - £63 = £6,167.

Activity 1.9 - Solution

The correct VAT payable by a business for the relevant VAT return period was £3,600. The VAT control account for the same period shows VAT payable of £3,045.

Identify which one of the following would explain this difference.

Output VAT of £555 was duplicated in the VAT control account	☐
Output VAT of £555 was omitted in the VAT control account	✓
Input VAT of £555 was omitted in the VAT control account	☐

- Output VAT of £555 was duplicated in the VAT control account. This includes £555 too much VAT being credited to the VAT control account (which would overstate the balance payable) so does not explain this difference.
- Output VAT of £555 was omitted in the VAT control account. If output VAT of £555 was omitted, then a lack of £555 being credited to the VAT control account would understate the balance payable. This is the correct answer.
- Input VAT of £555 was omitted in the VAT control account. If input VAT of £555 was omitted, then £555 too little would be debited (which would overstate the balance payable) so does not explain this difference.

Activity 1.10 - Solution

Accepting a task without possessing the adequate expertise or experience to carry out the task assigned would be a breach of Professional competence and due care.

Solutions to chapter 2 activities

Activity 2.1 - Solution

A business failed to register for VAT when it was required to do so. During this period, it made standard rated sales of £36,000.

If the business chooses to treat the invoices as VAT inclusive and absorb the VAT, the VAT amount would be:

£6000.

Standard rated sales £36,000 ÷ 120% x 20% = £6,000 VAT.

If the business chooses to recover the VAT from its customers, the VAT amount would be:

£7200.

Standard rated sales £36,000 ÷ 100% x 20% = £7,200 VAT.

Complete the following sentence.

The business may face a **Civil penalty** because it did not register for VAT when it is was required to do so.

Activity 2.2 - Solution

Show whether the following statements are true or false.

	TRUE	FALSE
It is mandatory for a business that makes wholly exempt supplies to follow MTD rules.	☐	✓
It is mandatory for a VAT-registered business with a taxable turnover above the VAT registration threshold to follow MTD rules.	✓	☐
It is mandatory for a VAT-registered business with a taxable turnover below the VAT registration threshold to follow MTD rules.	☐	✓

A business that makes wholly exempt supplies cannot register for VAT and therefore is not required to follow MTD rules for VAT. For a VAT-registered business with a taxable turnover above the VAT registration threshold, it is mandatory that it follows MTD rules. For a VAT-registered business with a taxable turnover below the VAT registration threshold (such as those businesses that have voluntarily registered for VAT), it is not currently mandatory to follow MTD rules (but the business can voluntarily sign up).

Activity 2.3 - Solution

Calculate the VAT payable to HMRC or reclaimable from HMRC for each business. Enter a negative figure if VAT is reclaimable from HMRC.

Business A

£-48000.

- Zero rated sales £350,000 to Business B (0% VAT charged).
- Standard rated purchases £240,000 excluding VAT. £240,000 ÷ 100% x 20% = £48,000 input VAT reclaimed.
- Business A will reclaim VAT from HMRC of £48,000.

Business B

£113000.

- Standard rated sales £750,000 inclusive of VAT to Business C. £750,000 ÷ 120% x 20% = £125,000 output VAT payable.
- Standard rated purchases £60,000 excluding VAT. £60,000 ÷ 100% x 20% = £12,000 input VAT reclaimed.
- Zero rated purchases £350,000 (0% VAT charged).
- Business B will pay VAT to HMRC of £113,000 (£125,000 output VAT - £12,000 input VAT).

Business C

£175000.

- Standard rated sales £1,500,000 excluding VAT to the general public. £1,500,000 ÷ 100% x 20% = £300,000 output VAT payable.
- Standard rated purchases £625,000 excluding VAT. £625,000 ÷ 100% x 20% = £125,000 input VAT reclaimed.
- Business C will pay VAT to HMRC of £175,000 (£300,000 output VAT - £125,000 input VAT).

Activity 2.4 - Solution

A business makes only zero-rated sales.

Show whether the following statements are true or false.

	TRUE	FALSE
Zero-rated goods and services count as taxable supplies and are part of taxable turnover.	✓	
The business cannot register for VAT.		✓
The business can apply to HMRC to be exempt from registering for VAT.	✓	

Activity 2.5 - Solution

A business is partly exempt for VAT purposes and has input VAT which it wants to reclaim for its VAT return. Input VAT in connection with taxable and exempt sales include the following:

	Input VAT
Standard Rated Supplies	£35,000
Zero Rated Supplies	£10,000
Exempt Supplies	£2,000

Input tax in relation to exempt supplies made is less than the de minimis limit.

Complete the following statement.

The amount of input VAT that can be reclaimed by the business is **All of it**.

A business that is registered for VAT but that makes some exempt supplies is referred to as partly exempt. If the amount of input tax incurred relating to exempt supplies is below the 'de minimus' amount, input tax can be reclaimed in full. If the amount of input tax incurred relating to exempt supplies is above the 'de minimus' amount, only input tax that relates to taxable (standard rated and zero rated) supplies can be reclaimed.

Activity 2.6 - Solution

A business started to trade on 1 January 20X5.

The business makes a mixture of sales for both standard-rated and exempt supplies. The business sales are spaced evenly throughout the year at £30,000 per month. 40% of all sales each month are exempt supplies.

By which month must the business apply to be registered for VAT.

31 March 20X5	☐
31 April 20X5	☐
31 May 20X5	✓

The VAT registration threshold includes only taxable (not exempt supplies). Standard-rated supplies are £18,000 per month (£30,000 x 60%). The business will exceed the current registration limit of £85,000 by 31 May 20X5 (Jan X5 to May X5 £18,000 x 5 months = £90,000) and must register within 30 days of 31 May 20X5.

Activity 2.7 - Solution

Which of the following is a non-taxable supply.

Zero-rated sales	☐
Reduced rate sales	☐
Exempt sales	✓
Standard rated sales	☐

Solutions to chapter 3 activities

Activity 3.1 - Solution

Which one of the following businesses is more likely to benefit from joining the flat rate scheme for VAT accounting.

A business that makes mainly standard rated sales	✓
A business that makes mainly zero rated sales	☐
A business that makes mainly exempt sales	☐

A business that makes mainly standard rated sales would charge high amounts of output VAT on its sales made to its customers. Joining the flat rate scheme could lower its VAT payable to HMRC.

A business that makes mainly zero-rated sales would regularly receive VAT repayments under normal VAT accounting rules. If joining the flat rate scheme, it would have to make VAT payments based on its total VAT-inclusive turnover, so it could be worse off.

A business that makes mainly exempt sales would charge little or no VAT on its sales made to its customers. Joining the flat rate scheme, it would have to make VAT payments based on its total VAT-inclusive turnover, so it could be worse off.

Activity 3.2 - Solution

The VAT return must be submitted to HMRC no later than **7 April 20X9**.

Assuming there are no weekends or bank holidays. HMRC will automatically collect payment from the business's bank account no earlier than **10 April 20X9**.

The VAT return must be submitted to HMRC by the 7 April 20X9 (28 February 20X9 + one calendar month later + extra seven days). The due date for VAT payment will also be 7 April 20X9. If the business pays HMRC by Direct Debit, HMRC will automatically collect payment from the business's bank account three working days after 7 April 20X9. Assuming no weekends or bank holidays (which are not working days) payment will be taken on 10 April 20X9 (7 April 20X9 + 3 working days).

Activity 3.3 - Solution

	TRUE	FALSE
Monthly returns can improve a business's cash flow, in particular when the business makes wholly or mainly zero-rated sales.	✓	
Monthly returns can improve a business's cash flow, in particular when the business makes wholly exempt sales.		✓
When using the annual accounting scheme for VAT a business normally submits one VAT Return a year and makes payments of VAT four times a year.		✓

Monthly returns can help with a business's cash flow, in particular when the business makes wholly or mainly zero-rated sales, because it is more likely to receive repayments of VAT from HMRC.

A business that makes wholly exempt sales cannot register for VAT.

When using the annual accounting scheme, the business submits one VAT Return per year, rather than four. After completing an annual VAT Return it settles any balance of VAT due two months after the VAT year end. The business makes nine fixed monthly payments in advance towards its yearly VAT bill.

Activity 3.4 - Solution

Which special accounting scheme for VAT is more likely beneficial to the business.

Flat rate scheme	☐
Cash accounting scheme	✓
Annual accounting scheme	☐

Using cash accounting may help improve cash flow, especially if customers are slow payers because payment of output VAT is not made until the business has received payment from the customer. If a business has a bad debt another benefit is that it will never need to pay the output VAT over to HMRC.

Activity 3.5 - Solution

Show whether the following statements are true or false.

	TRUE	FALSE
Businesses can start on the annual accounting scheme if their estimated taxable turnover during the next tax year is not more than £1.35 million.	✓	
Businesses can start on the flat rate accounting scheme if their estimated taxable turnover during the next tax year is not more than £1.35 million.		✓
A limited cost business is a business that typically has purchases that represent less than 2% of its sales turnover.	✓	

The second statement is false. A businesses can start on the flat rate accounting scheme if its VAT-exclusive taxable turnover is not more than £150,000 per year.

Activity 3.6 - Solution

A business is preparing its VAT return for the quarter ended 30 June 20X2. The following transactions were recorded in the previous three months.

- Sales invoices £120,000 plus VAT.
- Payments received from customers £210,000 plus VAT.
- Purchases invoices £40,000 plus VAT.
- Payments made to suppliers £90,000 plus VAT.

Based only on the information for the current VAT Return above, is the business better off using the cash accounting scheme. No.

Standard VAT accounting

- Sales invoices £120,000 x 20% VAT = £24,000.
- Purchases invoices £40,000 x 20% VAT = £8,000.
- VAT payable £16,000 (£24,000 - £8,000).

Cash accounting for VAT

- Payments received from customers £210,000 x 20% VAT = £42,000.
- Payments made to suppliers £90,000 x 20% VAT = £18,000.
- VAT payable £24,000 (£42,000 - £18,000).

The business would be £8,000 (£24,000 - £16,000) worse off in cash-flow, if it joined the cash accounting scheme.

Activity 3.7 - Solution

The VAT return must be submitted to HMRC and payment of any VAT due no later than **7 April 20X9**. 28 February 20X9 + one calendar month later + extra seven days = 7 April 20X9.

Solutions to chapter 4 activities

Activity 4.1 - Solution

Identify whether the following statements about the soft-landing period for record keeping and filing penalties under Making Tax Digital (MTD) are true or false.

	TRUE	FALSE
HMRC will allow a period of time for businesses to have in place digital links between all parts of their functional compatible software.	✓	
During the soft landing period, HMRC will not accept the use of 'cut and paste' or 'copy and paste' as being a digital link for VAT periods.		✓
HMRC's soft landing period to penalties would include late payment of VAT by the business.		✓

Activity 4.2 - Solution

A business submits its VAT Return late and has submitted its previous two VAT Returns late to HMRC.

Which one of the following statements is most likely correct.

The business would incur a surcharge	✓
A Surcharge Liability Notice would be issued by HMRC	
A surcharge is only issued by HMRC if the businesses VAT return is late again	
No action would be taken by HMRC	

A business may enter a 12-month 'surcharge period' if it defaults. The first default is dealt with by a warning known as a 'Surcharge Liability Notice'. This notice tells the business that if it submits its return or pays its VAT late again ('defaults') during the 12-month period (the surcharge period) then it may incur a surcharge.

If the business defaults again during the 12 months period, the surcharge period will be extended by a further 12 months and the business may have to pay a 'surcharge'. The surcharge is a percentage of the VAT outstanding on the due date for the accounting period that was in default. The surcharge percentage increases every time the business defaults in a surcharge period.

Activity 4.3 - Solution

A business has discovered an error from a previous VAT Return.

Identify for each of the circumstances explained below, whether the error can be corrected by adjusting the current VAT Return of the business (method 1), or whether the business would need to make a separate declaration to HMRC's VAT Error Correction Team in writing about the mistake (method 2).

	Method 1	Method 2
A careless error made of £55,000. The total sales of the business included in box 6 of its current VAT Return is £6 million excluding VAT.	☐	☑
A deliberate error made of £24,000. The total sales of the business included in box 6 of its current VAT Return is £1.2 million excluding VAT.	☐	☑
A careless error made of £45,000. The total sales of the business included in box 6 of its current VAT Return is £6 million excluding VAT.	☑	☐

- **A careless error made of £55,000. The total sales of the business included in box 6 of its current VAT Return is £6 million excluding VAT.**

The error is non-deliberate so the error reporting threshold may apply.

Error reporting threshold is the greater of:
- £10,000, or
- 1% of £6,000,000 (box 6 amount) on the current VAT Return. £6,000,000 ÷ 100% x 1% = £60,000 (subject to an upper limit of £50,000).

The greater of the two amounts above is £60,000 (not £10,000). However, the £60,000 has an upper limit of £50,000. The error reporting threshold is therefore £50,000.

The net value of all errors is £55,000 and is above the threshold of £50,000 therefore the business must separately declare to HMRC the errors and omissions and not make an adjustment on its current VAT Return (method 2).

- **A deliberate error made of £24,000. The total sales of the business included in box 6 of its current VAT Return is £1.2 million excluding VAT.**

The correction of deliberate inaccuracies must always be reported to HMRC's VAT Error Correction Team (method 2), regardless of the error reporting threshold.

- **A careless error made of £45,000. The total sales of the business included in box 6 of its current VAT Return is £6 million excluding VAT.**

The error is non-deliberate so the error reporting threshold may apply.

Error reporting threshold is the greater of:

- £10,000, or
- 1% of £6,000,000 (box 6 amount) on the current VAT Return. £6,000,000 ÷ 100% x 1% = £60,000 (subject to an upper limit of £50,000).

The greater of the two amounts above is £60,000 (not £10,000). However, the £60,000 has an upper limit of £50,000. The error reporting threshold is therefore £50,000.

The net value of all errors is £45,000 and is below the threshold of £50,000 therefore method 1 can be used, and the errors corrected by making an adjustment on the current VAT Return.

Activity 4.4 - Solution

Identify whether the following statements are true or false.

	TRUE	FALSE
A Surcharge Liability Notice would be issued for late payment of VAT.	✓	
A business will pay a penalty every time it is issued with a Surcharge Liability Notice.		✓
Deliberate VAT inaccuracies are a criminal offence and carry a possible prison sentence.	✓	

A surcharge means an additional charge (penalty). The notice tells the business that if it submits its VAT return, or pays its VAT late again during the next 12-month period (the surcharge period), it may incur a surcharge. The second statement is false because the business does not incur a surcharge (penalty) on its first default.

Activity 4.5 - Solution

Identify whether the following circumstances will normally incur a penalty or not incur a penalty for a business.

	Penalty	No Penalty
Careless errors that are discovered from a previous VAT Return	✓	☐
Late VAT registration by a business	✓	☐
A business does not have full digital links between its software programs to submit its VAT Returns	☐	✓

Careless or deliberate VAT errors discovered from previous VAT Returns are liable to a penalty. HMRC may charge a civil penalty if a business fails to notify them on time that it should be registered for VAT. The amount of penalty charged will depend on the amount of VAT due and how late the business registered. The soft-landing period (also called light touch approach) by HMRC will allow a period of time (a soft-landing period) for businesses to have in place digital links between all parts of their functional compatible software.

Solutions to chapter 5 activities

Activity 5.1 - Solution

Identify whether the following statements about simplified invoices are true or false.

	TRUE	FALSE
A simplified invoice can be issued only when the VAT inclusive amount of a sale is less than £25.	☐	☑
A simplified invoice must show the rate of VAT charged for each item sold.	☑	☐
A simple till receipt can be assumed to be acceptable as a simplified invoice for reclaiming VAT.	☐	☑

A simplified (less detailed) invoice can be issued only when the VAT inclusive amount of a sale is less than £250 (not £25). A simple till receipt is not acceptable as a valid VAT invoice to reclaim VAT. A simplified invoice must show the rate of VAT charged for each item sold.

Activity 5.2 - Solution

Complete the following sentence.

The actual tax point for the sale of goods is **7 January 20X9**.

The time of supply rules is not used for the VAT Cash Accounting Scheme, the tax point to account for VAT is always the date that payment is received, or payment is made.

Activity 5.3 - Solution

Use drag and drop to identify the most likely tax point for the 20% deposit paid in advance and tax point for the final payment.

20% deposit	Final payment
14 December 20X8	7 January 20X9

Tax point for the 20% deposit:

- The date the goods were ordered is not relevant.
- Date of supply 7 January 20X9.
- Date of payment for deposit 14 December 20X8.

The earliest date shown above for the 20% deposit is the date of payment on 14 December 20X8 which is therefore the actual tax point. 14 December 20X8 determines the correct VAT Return period to account for the VAT for the 20% deposit.

Tax point for the final payment:

- The date the goods were ordered is not relevant.
- Date of supply 7 January 20X9.

The earliest date shown above is the date of supply on 7 January 20X9 which is the basic tax point. Whenever the basic tax point has been selected you then need to check that the '14-day rule' for invoicing does or does not apply. Based solely on the information provided an invoice has not been provided, therefore 7 January 20X9 would determine the correct VAT Return period to account for the final payment.

Activity 5.4 - Solution

Goods were collected by a customer on 7 June 20X9. The business invoiced the customer for the goods on 5 May 20X9. Payment for the goods was made by the customer on 7 May 20X9.

Identify the correct VAT Return when the transaction should be included.

VAT Return quarter ending 30 November 20X8	☐
VAT Return quarter ending 28 February 20X9	☐
VAT Return quarter ending 31 May 20X9	✓
VAT Return quarter ending 31 August 20X9	☐

- Date of supply 7 June 20X9.
- Date of invoice 5 May 20X9.
- Date of payment 7 May 20X9.

The earliest date shown above is the date of invoice on 5 May 20X9 which is therefore the actual tax point. 5 May 20X9 determines the correct VAT Return period to account for the VAT which would be the quarter ending 31 May 20X9.

Activity 5.5 - Solution

Identify whether the following documents are a valid VAT invoice or not a valid VAT invoice.

	Valid VAT invoice	Not a valid VAT invoice
Pro-forma invoice	☐	✓
Invoice for only zero-rated or exempt supplies	☐	✓
Simplified invoice	✓	☐

Activity 5.6 - Solution

A VAT registered business supplies to a customer, standard rated goods worth £200 and £25 worth of goods that are exempt for VAT purposes.

Complete the following sentence.

The business **cannot** issue a simplified VAT invoice.

A simplified (less detailed) invoice can be issued when the VAT inclusive amount of a sale is less than £250. A simplified invoice cannot be issued if the sale includes exempt supplies.

Activity 5.7 - Solution

Goods were sent to a customer on 18 December 20X2. The business invoiced the customer for the goods on 29 December 20X2. Payment was made by the customer on 7 January 20X3.

Complete the following sentence.

The actual tax point for the sale of goods is **29 December 20X2**.

- Date of supply 18 December 20X2.
- Date of invoice 29 December 20X2.
- Date of payment 7 January 20X3.

The earliest date shown above is the date of supply on 18 December 20X2 which is the basic tax point. Whenever the basic tax point has been selected you then need to check that the '14-day rule' for invoicing does or does not apply.

The latest the invoice should be sent for the 14-day rule to apply would be by 31 December 20X2 (within 14 days of the basic tax point on 18 December 20X2). The invoice was sent on 29 December 20X2 and is within 14 days of the basic tax point, the invoice date 29 December 20X2 becomes the actual tax point that determines the correct VAT Return period to account for the VAT.

Solution to chapter 6 activities

Activity 6.1 - Solution

Identify whether the following statements are true or false.

	TRUE	FALSE
A VAT registered business can normally reclaim VAT on the purchase price of a new car, if the car is used for self drive hire by its customers.	✓	☐
A VAT registered business can normally reclaim VAT on the purchase of commercial vehicles, such as lorries or vans.	✓	☐
A business can normally reclaim all VAT it pays on private fuel used, for company vehicles driven by employees.	☐	✓

The last statement is false, there is no method that allows full recovery of input VAT paid on private fuel used, the business either does not reclaim any input VAT, reclaims only the proportion of input VAT that relates to business use, or pays a fuel scale charge which reduces the input VAT it has reclaimed.

Activity 6.2 - Solution

A business is partly exempt for VAT purposes and has input VAT which it wants to reclaim for its current VAT return. Input VAT paid in connection with taxable and exempt supplies include the following:

	Input VAT
Standard Rated Supplies	£3,701
Zero Rated Supplies	£2,444
Exempt Supplies	£8,772

Input tax that relates to exempt supplies is more than the de minimis limit.

Complete the following sentence.

The amount of input VAT that can be reclaimed by the business is **Some of it**.

A business that makes taxable and non-taxable (exempt) supplies is referred to as 'partly exempt'. If the amount of input tax that relates to exempt supplies is less than (or equal to) the 'de minimus' amount, the input tax can be reclaimed in full. If the amount of input tax that relates to exempt supplies is more than the 'de minimus' amount, the input tax cannot be reclaimed.

£3,701 and £2,444 input VAT can ALL be reclaimed because the input VAT relates to taxable supplies. The amount of input tax that relates to exempt supplies (£8,772) is stated as more than the 'de minimus' amount, therefore the £8,772 input tax cannot be reclaimed.

Activity 6.3 - Solution

A business held an annual party and invited its customers, suppliers, employees and any guests.

Complete the following sentence.

The amount of input VAT that can be reclaimed by the business is **Some of it**.

When the nature of entertainment is for a mixture of persons, the business can only reclaim input VAT paid on the proportion of expenditure that relates to employees and overseas customers only.

Activity 6.4

A business is preparing its VAT return and needs to calculate VAT reclaimed on fuel used by an employee, that has driven a business car for private use.

- Total input VAT paid on fuel for the car in the relevant VAT period was £16.67.
- The fuel scale charge for the car for the relevant VAT period is £150 including VAT.

Calculate the net amount of VAT payable or reclaimed by the business, if it uses fuel scale charges to account for VAT on private fuel. Do not use a minus sign or brackets. Round your answer to two decimal places.

£8.33.

- Total input VAT paid on fuel for the VAT period was £16.67.
- The relevant fuel scale charge relating to the car is £150 including VAT for the VAT period. £150 ÷ 120% x 20% VAT = £25.00.
- Output tax £25.00 - Input tax £16.67 = £8.33 VAT payable.

Activity 6.5 - Solution

A business operates no special accounting schemes for VAT. It supplied standard rated goods to a customer and invoiced them for £2,000 plus VAT on 2 February 20X2. The invoice was due to be paid by 4 March 20X2. All conditions for claiming bad debt relief have been met.

Identify which VAT Return gives the earliest opportunity for the business to claim bad debt relief.

VAT period ending 31 January 20X2	☐
VAT period ending 30 April 20X2	☐
VAT period ending 31 July 20X2	☐
VAT period ending 31 October 20X2	✓

To claim bad debt relief the debt needs to be more than six months old (and less than four years and six months old) from the later of when payment of the invoice was due (4 March 20X2), or the date of supply (2 February 20X2). The latest of the two dates is 4 March 20X2, so plus 6 months = 3 September 20X2, this is the earliest date that bad debt relief can be claimed. 3 September 20X2 falls within the relevant VAT period ending 31 October 20X2.

Activity 6.6 - Solution

Identify for each of the following types of expenditure, whether a business can normally reclaim all input VAT or reclaim no input VAT.

	Reclaim ALL input VAT	Reclaim NO input VAT
Staff entertainment expenditure paid for by the business.	✓	☐
Repairs and maintenance costs for a business van.	✓	☐
The purchase of a new car by the business, that will be driven sometimes privately by an employee.	☐	✓

Activity 6.7 - Solution

Identify whether each of the following statements are true or false.

	TRUE	FALSE
A business can normally recover input VAT in connection with employee travel and subsistence.	✓	☐
Input VAT paid for entertaining UK customers, can normally be reclaimed by a VAT registered business.	☐	✓
A business entertains staff and one guest only for each member of staff at a Christmas party, all input VAT is reclaimable.	☐	✓

The second statement is false. A business can only reclaim input VAT paid on entertainment that relates to employees and overseas customers only, not UK customers.

The third statement is false. When the nature of entertainment is for a mixture of persons, the business can only reclaim input VAT paid on the proportion of expenditure that relates to employees and overseas customers only. Input VAT would not be reclaimed for the guests that attended with members of staff.

Solutions to chapter 7 activities

Activity 7.1 - Solution

Complete the following sentence.

A reverse charge is when a **seller** does not charge VAT on the invoice and the **buyer** would account for the input tax and output tax on their VAT return.

Activity 7.2 - Solution

Identify whether the following statements about reverse charges are true or false.

	TRUE	FALSE
Under the reverse charge mechanism, a seller will send an invoice to the buyer without VAT charged.	✓	
The seller would report the same VAT amount as both input VAT and output VAT on their VAT Return.		✓
Reverse charges have no effect on the sellers or buyers cash flow.	✓	

The buyer (not seller) would report the same VAT amount as both input VAT and output VAT on their VAT Return. Reverse charges have no effect on the sellers or buyers cash flow because no VAT is actually paid.

Activity 7.3 - Solution

Complete the following sentence.

When a UK VAT registered business supplies services to an overseas business, if the place of supply is overseas the sale is usually **Outside the scope of VAT**.

When the customer is a business customer (B2B) the place of supply is where the customer is (overseas), in which case no VAT is charged, and the supply is 'outside the scope' of UK VAT. This means the transaction is not accounted for on a VAT Return.

Activity 7.4 - Solution

Complete the following sentences.

Exports are goods supplied to overseas customers outside the EU.

Dispatches are goods supplied to overseas customers in an EU member state.

Solutions to chapter 8 activities

Activity 8.1 - Solution

(a) Enter the relevant figures into the on-line VAT Return for the period ended 31 December. Do not leave any box blank.

Exam note: Answers can show figures rounded up or rounded down. Both options are equally valid for the purposes of your exam assessment.

The double entry to record transactions in a sales and purchases account would always be excluding VAT.

On-line VAT Return for period ended 31 December		
Please note: Enter values in pounds sterling, including pence, for example 1000.00, except where indicated.		
VAT due in this period on sales and other outputs (Box 1)	24384.58 + 2478.13 =	26862.71
VAT due in this period on acquisitions from other EC member states (Box 2)	5000 x 20% VAT (reverse charge)	1000.00
Total VAT due (the sum of boxes 1 and 2) (Box 3)		Calculated value
VAT reclaimed in the period on purchases and other inputs (including acquisitions from the EC) (Box 4)	6984.57 + 996.32 + (5000 x 20% VAT) =	8980.89
Net VAT to be paid to HM Revenue & Customs or reclaimed by you (difference between boxes 3 and 4) (Box 5)		Calculated value
Total value of sales and all other outputs excluding any VAT. Include your Box 8 figure. (Box 6)	Total sales from the sales account	134313
Total value of purchases and all other inputs excluding any VAT. Include your Box 9 figure. (Box 7)	Total purchases from the purchases account	44904
Total value of all supplies of goods and related costs, excluding any VAT, to other EC member states (Box 8)	None	0
Total value of all acquisitions of goods and related costs, excluding any VAT, to other EC member states (Box 9)	EU purchases from the purchases account	5000

(b) Calculate the values that will be shown on-line when you submit the VAT Return for the following boxes. If a repayment is due, use a minus sign in Box 5. Enter the values in pounds sterling, including pence.

	Total VAT due (the sum of boxes 1 and 2) (Box 3)	26862.71 + 1000.00 =	27862.71
	Net VAT to be paid to HM Revenue & Customs or reclaimed by you (difference between boxes 3 and 4) (Box 5)	27862.71 - 8980.89 =	18881.82

Activity 8.2 - Solution

(a) Enter the relevant figures into the on-line VAT Return for the period ended 31 May.
Do not leave any box blank.

Exam note: Answers can show figures rounded up or rounded down. Both options are equally valid for the purposes of your exam assessment.

On-line VAT Return for period ended 31 May		
Please note: Enter values in pounds sterling, including pence, for example 1000.00, except where indicated.		
VAT due in this period on sales and other outputs (Box 1)	9194.84 - 110.00 - 115.20 + (22400 x 20%) =	13449.64
VAT due in this period on acquisitions from other EC member states (Box 2)	None	0.00
Total VAT due (the sum of boxes 1 and 2) (Box 3)		Calculated value
VAT reclaimed in the period on purchases and other inputs (including acquisitions from the EC) (Box 4)	1572.49 - 59.12 - 4.72 + 418.02 =	1926.67
Net VAT to be paid to HM Revenue & Customs or reclaimed by you (difference between boxes 3 and 4) (Box 5)		Calculated value
Total value of sales and all other outputs excluding any VAT. Include your Box 8 figure. (Box 6)	47999.22 - 550.00 - 575.99 + 22400.00 =	69273
Total value of purchases and all other inputs excluding any VAT. Include your Box 9 figure. (Box 7)	7862.47 - 295.60 - 23.58 + 2090.13 =	9633
Total value of all supplies of goods and related costs, excluding any VAT, to other EC member states (Box 8)	None	0
Total value of all acquisitions of goods and related costs, excluding any VAT, to other EC member states (Box 9)	None	0

(b) Calculate the values that will be shown on-line when you submit the VAT Return for the following boxes. If a repayment is due, use a minus sign in Box 5. Enter the values in pounds sterling, including pence.

Total VAT due (the sum of boxes 1 and 2) (Box 3)	Box 1 (13449.64) + Box 2 (0) =	13449.64
Net VAT to be paid to HM Revenue & Customs or reclaimed by you (difference between boxes 3 and 4) (Box 5)	13449.64 - 1926.67 =	11522.97

Activity 8.3 - Solution

(a) Enter the relevant figures into the on-line VAT Return for the period ended 30 April.
Do not leave any box blank.

Exam note: Answers can show figures rounded up or rounded down. Both options are equally valid for the purposes of your exam assessment.

The double entry to record transactions in a sales and purchases account would always be excluding VAT.

On-line VAT Return for period ended 30 April		
Please note: Enter values in pounds sterling, including pence, for example 1000.00, except where indicated.		
VAT due in this period on sales and other outputs (Box 1)	18194.42 + 1060.19 =	19254.61
VAT due in this period on acquisitions from other EC member states (Box 2)	None	0.00
Total VAT due (the sum of boxes 1 and 2) (Box 3)		Calculated value
VAT reclaimed in the period on purchases and other inputs (including acquisitions from the EC) (Box 4)	21984.56 + 1416.35 =	23400.91
Net VAT to be paid to HM Revenue & Customs or reclaimed by you (difference between boxes 3 and 4) (Box 5)		Calculated value
Total value of sales and all other outputs excluding any VAT. Include your Box 8 figure. (Box 6)	Total sales from the sales account	108663
Total value of purchases and all other inputs excluding any VAT. Include your Box 9 figure. (Box 7)	Total purchases from the purchases account	117005
Total value of all supplies of goods and related costs, excluding any VAT, to other EC member states (Box 8)	EU sales from the sales account	12390
Total value of all acquisitions of goods and related costs, excluding any VAT, to other EC member states (Box 9)	None	0

(b) Calculate the values that will be shown on-line when you submit the VAT Return for the following boxes. If a repayment is due, use a minus sign in Box 5. Enter the values in pounds sterling, including pence.

Total VAT due (the sum of boxes 1 and 2) (Box 3)	Box 1 (19254.61) + Box 2 (0) =	19254.61
Net VAT to be paid to HM Revenue & Customs or reclaimed by you (difference between boxes 3 and 4) (Box 5)	19254.61 - 23400.91 =	-4146.30

Activity 8.4 - Solution

Complete the following e-mail to the owner of the business.

To: Owner of the business
From: Accounting Technician
Date Wednesday 24 June
Subject: Completed VAT Return

Please be advised that the VAT Return for the period ended 31 May has been completed.

The amount of VAT **Payable** will be £**3,686.14**.

Please allow sufficient funds to permit HMRC to direct debit your account on **Friday 10 July**.

Kind regards,

Accounting Technician

VAT payable

Box 1 (£11,150.71) + Box 2 (£1,000.00) = £12,150.71 - Box 4 (£8,464.57) = £3,686.14.

The normal due date for submitting each VAT Return and electronically paying HMRC any VAT that is owed is one calendar month after the end of the relevant VAT period. Online filing and electronic payment mean that businesses get an extended due date for filing the return of seven extra calendar days after the normal due date shown on the VAT Return.

- VAT period ended 31 May.
- The business has one calendar month and 7 days after 31 May to file and pay its VAT.
- Today is Wednesday 24 June, Tuesday 30 June is one calendar month after 31 May.
- 7 days after Tuesday 30 June, is Tuesday 7 July. This is the deadline to submit the VAT Return and pay any VAT due.
- However, if the business pays HMRC by Direct Debit, HMRC automatically collects payment from the business's bank account three bank working days after the extra seven calendar days following the normal due date.
- The deadline to submit the VAT Return and pay any VAT due is Tuesday 7 July, therefore HMRC should automatically collect payment by direct debit on Friday 10 July.

Activity 8.5 - Solution

Complete the following e-mail to the owner of the business.

To: Owner of the business
From: Accounting Technician
Date Wednesday 29 July
Subject: VAT Return using the flat rate scheme for VAT

Please be advised that the VAT Return for the period ended 30 June has been completed.

The amount of VAT **Payable** will be £**4092**.

Please ensure the amount of any VAT due is paid by **Friday 7 August**.

The business can use the flat rate scheme for VAT if its VAT **Exclusive** taxable turnover is less than £150,000 per year, the business could simplify its VAT accounting by registering on the Flat Rate Scheme and calculating VAT payments as a percentage of its total VAT **Inclusive** turnover.

Once on the flat rate scheme, the business can continue to use it until its total business income exceeds £**230,000**.

Kind regards,

Accounting Technician

The amount of VAT payable by the business for its current VAT return is £4,092.
- The VAT payment would be 11% of its total VAT-inclusive turnover.
- Total VAT-inclusive turnover is £37,200 (£26,000 standard rated sales plus VAT 20% = £31,200 + £6,000 zero rated sales).
- £37,200 x 11% = VAT payable £4,092.
- The business does not reclaim input VAT on its purchases if using the flat rate scheme.

The normal due date for submitting each VAT Return and electronically paying HMRC any VAT that is owed is one calendar month after the end of the relevant VAT period. Online filing and electronic payment mean that businesses get an extended due date for filing the return of seven extra calendar days after the normal due date shown on the VAT Return.

Activity 8.6 - Solution

Answers can be rounded up or rounded down. Both options are equally valid for the purposes of your assessment. The double entry to record transactions in a sales and purchases account would always be excluding VAT.

(a) Calculate the figure that should be included in box 1 of the VAT Return, once any necessary corrections have been made to the ledger accounts. Enter your figure in pounds sterling, including pence.

£10713.47.

(b) Calculate the figure that should be included in box 4 of the VAT Return, once any necessary corrections have been made to the ledger accounts. Enter your figure in pounds sterling, including pence.

£7594.32.

(c) Calculate the figure that should be included in box 6 of the VAT Return, once any necessary corrections have been made to the ledger accounts. Enter your figure in whole pounds only.

£53367.

VAT due in this period on sales and other outputs **(Box 1)**	10304.58 + 500.00 - 131.11 + 40.00 VAT on fuel scale charge =	10713.47
VAT reclaimed in the period on purchases and other inputs (including acquisitions from the EC) **(Box 4)**	8304.56 - 710.24 =	7594.32
Total value of sales and all other outputs excluding any VAT. Include your Box 8 figure. **(Box 6)**	Total net sales from the sales account 53367.35 + net fuel scale charge 200 + omitted invoice 2400 =	53367

The relevant HMRC fuel scale charge for the VAT period is £240 including VAT.

- £240 x 1/6 = £40 output VAT declared in Box 1.
- £240 x 5/6 = £200 net sale declared in Box 6.

Fuel scale charges are the equivalent of a sales invoice raised for the cost of private fuel used by the employee (although the employee is not expected to pay it). By accounting for VAT using fuel scale charges, the business can then reclaim 100% of all VAT paid on fuel, including private fuel.

A sales invoice for £2,400 excluding VAT has been omitted from the accounting records shown above, the goods sold were zero-rated supplies. Increase Box 6 by £2,400, there is no VAT to account for so no Box 1 entry.

Activity 8.7 - Solution

Answers can be rounded up or rounded down. Both options are equally valid for the purposes of your assessment. The double entry to record transactions in a sales and purchases account would always be excluding VAT.

VAT on omitted invoices:

- Sales invoice for £2,800 excluding VAT x 20% = £560 output VAT.
- Purchases invoice for £450 excluding VAT x 20% = £90 input VAT.
- £560 output VAT - £90 input VAT = £470 net output VAT due.

(a) Calculate the net value of all errors used to adjust the current VAT Return. Enter your figure in pounds sterling, including pence.

£470.00.

If input VAT and output VAT errors are discovered from a previous VAT Return in the same exercise, the net value of all the errors is used to adjust the VAT liability on the VAT Return. Either Box 1 or Box 4 is adjusted, as appropriate. If the business discovers that it did not account for output VAT to HMRC of £560 on a supply made in the past, and also did not account for £90 input VAT reclaimable on a purchase, it should add £470 to the Box 1 figure for output VAT on the current VAT Return.

(b) Calculate the figure that should be included in box 1 of the VAT Return, once any necessary corrections have been made to the ledger accounts. Enter your figure in pounds sterling, including pence.

£12334.61.

(c) Calculate the figure that should be included in box 4 of the VAT Return, once any necessary corrections have been made to the ledger accounts. Enter your figure in pounds sterling, including pence.

£9000.91.

VAT due in this period on sales and other outputs **(Box 1)**	11194.42 + 670.19 + error from prvious return 470 =	12334.61
VAT reclaimed in the period on purchases and other inputs (including acquisitions from the EC) **(Box 4)**	7984.56 + 1016.35 =	9000.91

Activity 8.8 - Solution

A business made a non-careless and non-deliberate error on a previous VAT Return.

- VAT of £56 on a purchase invoice from a UK supplier was omitted in the accounting records.
- VAT of £8 on a credit note from a UK supplier was duplicated in the accounting records.

The business is allowed to correct the net error on its current VAT Return.

Which one of the following corrections should the business make in Box 4 of its current VAT Return.

Add £64	✓
Add £48	☐
Deduct £64	☐
Deduct £48	☐

- VAT of £56 on a purchase invoice from a UK supplier was omitted in the accounting records. This is input VAT that should have been added to Box 4 in a previous VAT return to increase input VAT reclaimed. Add £56 to Box 4.
- VAT of £8 on a credit note from a UK supplier was duplicated in the accounting records. This is input VAT that was deducted from Box 4 in a previous VAT return to decrease input VAT reclaimed. It was deducted twice in error therefore add back £8 to Box 4.
- Add £56 and £8 to Box 4 (total amount £56 + £8 = £64).

Printed in Great Britain
by Amazon